English
for
Science and Technology Students

— Developing Skills for Scientific Communication —

Asahi Press

音声再生アプリ「リスニング・トレーナー」を使った音声ダウンロード

朝日出版社開発のアプリ、「リスニング・トレーナー（リストレ）」を使えば、教科書の音声をスマホ、タブレットに簡単にダウンロードできます。どうぞご活用ください。

◉ アプリ【リスニング・トレーナー】の使い方

《アプリのダウンロード》

App Store または Google Play から「リスニング・トレーナー」のアプリ（無料）をダウンロード

App Storeはこちら▶

Google Playはこちら▶

《アプリの使い方》

① アプリを開き「コンテンツを追加」をタップ
② 画面上部に【15653】を入力しDoneをタップ

音声ストリーミング配信 》》》

この教科書の音声は、右記ウェブサイトにて無料で配信しています。

 https://text.asahipress.com/free/english/

表紙：DC カンパニー
写真：iStock.com
　　　Shutterstock

はしがき

　最近の大学教育を取り巻く環境は大きく変化しています。大学教育の質保証、学修成果の可視化の重要性が強調されています。英語教育においても、4技能重視、アクティブラーニングといった学び方、評価におけるルーブリックの活用など学習環境が大きく変わってきています。

　このテキストでは、理工系の大学生、高専生を対象に、科学的な英文を読むために必要な語彙、文法の基礎力を身につけ、さらに聞く力・発信型の書く力、話す力を伸ばす演習を組み込んでいます。

　具体的にどのように到達目標に達成できるか、実際の外部試験に準拠した演習を行いながら、単語の覚え方から和訳に必要な知識の整理まで学習方略にも焦点をあてています。英文を読み問題を解いて学習内容を確認・定着させるだけでなく、それぞれの Unit の英文を読むことでどのような語彙力、文法力、そして聞く、話す力まで身についたのか学習成果が可視化できるように演習に配列に工夫をしたつもりです。

　ぜひ、辞書を引いて、単語の意味を確認するなど初歩的な学習方法に立ち返りながら、理工系の専門に関する英文を読み進めていく中で4技能の力を伸ばしてください。このテキストを読み終えたときに、工業英検などの実際に外部の資格試験で力を試して学習成果を実感してもらえれば幸いです。

著者一同

Contents

Do you have what it takes?

必要な資質は持っていますか。

到達目標
□ 英和辞典をひくことができる。
□ 名詞について説明できる。
□ 主語について説明できる。
□ 技術者、科学者の資質や仕事について説明できる。

事前学習 次の単語や熟語を予習して授業を受けましょう。

A 次の(1)から(10)の名詞(事物の名前)の訳として最も適切な日本語をそれぞれ①から③より、選びなさい。

____ (1) architect   [① 建築家   ② 専門家   ③ 芸術家]
____ (2) quality   [① 質量   ② 資質   ③ 原料]
____ (3) solution   [① 特性   ② 解決   ③ 問題]
____ (4) concern   [① 懸念   ② 決算   ③ 予算]
____ (5) efficiency   [① 効率   ② 実用   ③ 進化]
____ (6) emission   [① 吸入   ② 消化   ③ 排出]
____ (7) fuel   [① 道具   ② 摩擦   ③ 燃料]
____ (8) reduction   [① 現象   ② 削減   ③ 導体]
____ (9) creativity   [① 工業化   ② 想像   ③ 創造力]
____ (10) cooperation   [① 協力   ② 強化   ③ 電流]

B 次の(1)から(5)の英文に入れる語として最適なものを下の①から⑤より選びなさい。なお、①から⑤は1回しか使えません。

____ (1) Thanks (　　　) engineers' efforts, we have hybrid cars with low emissions.

____ (2) We should come up (　　　) unique ideas and solutions.

____ (3) (　　　) the other hand, they could also cause a serious problem.

____ (4) Engineers are good (　　　) science and math.

____ (5) (　　　) example, the concern for fuel efficiency was a problem.

[① For   ② with   ③ at   ④ On   ⑤ to]

(2)   Sit back and close your eyes. Think. No dream. Dream about your future and what you want to be and do. Do you want to be a scientist? An architect? An engineer? One of these careers may be a part of your dream, but do you have what it takes to become a scientist, an architect or an engineer? Let's see.   5

   You may think that you only need to be good at science and math to be an engineer or scientist. Those qualities are of course very important, but they may not be the most important qualities or characteristics of a good engineer or scientist.

   Engineers and scientists are people that see problems in the   10
world and then try to come up with a solution for those problems. For example, as more and more people have begun to drive cars, the concern for fuel efficiency and reduction in emission gases have become problems. These problems need solutions, and engineers have helped. Today we have hybrid cars with   15
low emissions, electric cars, and solar powered cars with solar-paneled highways.

(3)   Good engineers are also creative. They think "out of the box" to come up with unique ideas and solutions. Creativity and ingenious ideas have brought us the computer, the smart phone   20
and the Internet. A whole new digital world has brought sights, sounds and information from all over the world to our finger-tips. And as our computers and tablets become smaller, lighter and as the Internet becomes faster, engineers and scientists are now preparing for a post-Digital Age.   25

Good engineers are also very careful with detail. A miscalculation or a mistake sometimes is a way to find a new solution or a new product. But on the other hand, a miscalculation or a mistake could also become a serious problem.

30 For that reason, engineers need to be meticulous, cautious and careful while still being creative and adventuresome when it comes to solving problems.

4 Engineers need to be able to communicate well with others. Many engineers work alone when they design something.

35 However, if they want their design to be used by others, they will need to be able to speak to clients or other engineers about their designs. They must communicate their ideas effectively. Team-work is also very important for engineers. Cooperation and collaboration are also important parts of an engineer's work.

40 So as you can see, just being good at mathematics and science is not all that is necessary to be a good engineer. Careers in engineering are demanding but very rewarding, and as an engineer you truly can help to solve today's problems for tomorrow's world. Do you have what it takes?

(442 words)

Notes

l. 2　what you want to be and do　何になりたくて何をしたいか

l. 4　what it takes (to)　(…に)なるための資質、技能

l. 7　of course　もちろん

l. 11　those problems　これらの問題とはあとに続く、多くの人々が車の運転を始めると燃料効率や排ガス規制など。

l. 31　adventuresome ＝ adventurous 冒険的な、冒険好きの

1 次の(1)から(5)に続くフレーズとして最も適切なものを下の①から⑤より選びなさい。なお、①から⑤は1回しか使えません。

____ (1) Does your career

____ (2) To be good at science

____ (3) More and more people began to

____ (4) A new digital world has

____ (5) Engineers are now

① may not be the most important characteristic.

② brought information from all over the world.

③ preparing for a post-Digital Age.

④ use computers.

⑤ fit you and your personality?

2 次の(1)から(5)の英文がそれぞれ正しい意味を表すように、和文を参考にして( )に入れる最も適切な語を下の①から⑩より選びなさい。なお、①から⑩は1回しか使えません。

____ (1) 座って目を閉じてごらんなさい。

( ) back and close your eyes.

____ (2) 私たちはとても細かいところまで注意すべきです。

We should be careful with ( ).

____ (3) 問題を解くとなると創造的にならないといけません。

We have to be creative when it comes to ( ) problems.

____ (4) 多くの技術者は何かデザインをするときには自分たちだけで仕事をします。

Many engineers work ( ) when they design something.

____ (5) 人々は自分たちのアイデアを効率よく伝えるべきです。

They should communicate their ideas ( ).

① difficulty	② solving	③ alone	④ Sit	⑤ detail
⑥ themselves	⑦ effectively	⑧ effect	⑨ Seat	⑩ solves

3 次の(1)から(5)までの英文で本文の内容に合致しているものには ① (= true)を、異なっているものは ② (= false)を書きなさい。

____ (1) To be a good engineer or scientist, you must study only math harder.

____ (2) A good engineer or scientist does not have to communicate with other scientists.

____ (3) To solve problems, engineers need creativity and ingenious ideas.

____ (4) Engineers and scientists are trying to find solutions.

____ (5) Engineers and scientists want their designs to be used by other engineers.

4 〈主語〉（主語 = Subject「～は、～が、～も」にあたる語句で、名詞、代名詞、名詞句、名詞節が主語になります）それぞれの英文の主語に注意して下線部の空所に適切な日本語を書き入れなさい。

(1) Does one of these careers fit you and your personality?

_____ は、あなたやあなたの個性にぴったりしているのでしょうか。

(2) Good engineers and scientists are also creative.

_____ は、また創造的でもあります。

(3) The concern for fuel efficiency and reduction in emission gases were problems.

_____ は、問題でした。

(4) Just being good at mathematics and science is not all that is necessary to be a good engineer or scientist.

_____ は、よい技術者や科学者になるために必要なすべてではありません。

(5) A whole new digital world has brought sights, sounds and information from all over the world to our finger-tips.

_____ が、世界中の光景や音声、情報を私たちの指先までもたらしてくれました。

Discussion, Paragraph Writing, Presentation

Questions for Discussion

1. Think of a famous engineer or scientist? Why are they famous? What traits do they have?

2. What traits are important for a good friend? Teacher? Boss?

3. Who in your group is a good listener? Who is creative? Who is good at solving problems?

4. Discuss with your group the various traits that make a good scientist or engineer? Who in your group would make a great engineer or scientist? Why?

Pair Dictation ペアになって偶数・奇数の文を読みあって、書き取りなさい。

A 1. My best friend is great at mathematics.
   3. Joe is a great listener, and he is always calm.
   5. Becky is a great team member. She is so supportive.

B 2. My dad is an engineer, and he is very careful with detail.
   4. My professor speaks English, German and Chinese.
   6. I am shy, so it is hard to speak in front of other people.

Presentation

Give a 20 to 30 second self-introduction. Include where you are from and what your strong personality traits are.

Hello, my name is ......

I am from ......

In high school, I really liked my ...... class / club. I am strong in ......

I like to (solve problems, program computers, do experiments).

In the future I want to become a ......

Thank you for listening.

English Learning and AI

英語学習と人工知能

到達目標
□ 動詞について説明できる。
□ 人工知能について説明できる。
□ 人工知能と英語学習の関係について説明できる。

事前学習 次の単語や熟語を予習して授業を受けましょう。

A 次の(1)から(10)の動詞(動作や状態を表す品詞で時制や進行相、完了相、分詞、不定詞、動名詞など様々な活用をする)の訳として最も適切な日本語をそれぞれ①から③より、選びなさい。

____ (1) access [① 接近する ② 接続する ③ 接着する]
____ (2) translate [① 翻訳する ② 移動する ③ 変換する]
____ (3) market [① 建てる ② 壊す ③ 市場で売買する]
____ (4) sell [① 買う ② 売る ③ 借りる]
____ (5) code [① プログラム化する ② 線をつなぐ ③ 記憶する]
____ (6) determine [① 決定する ② 消化する ③ 排出する]
____ (7) replace [① 直す ② 置き換える ③ 使用する]
____ (8) change [① 削減する ② 増加する ③ 変化する]
____ (9) remain [① 思い出す ② 残る ③ 創造する]
____ (10) compose [① 協力する ② 校正する ③ 作曲する]

B 次の(1)から(5)の英文に入れる語として最適なものを下の ① から ⑤ より選びなさい。なお、① から ⑤ は1回しか使えません。

____ (1) Please look (　　　) the meaning of the word in the dictionary when you don't know it.

____ (2) Intelligent devices have been creeping (　　　) the classroom.

____ (3) They are based (　　　) an application of Artificial Intelligence.

____ (4) This music is similar (　　　) that one.

____ (5) Students speak (　　　) others in a foreign language.

[① to ② with ③ into ④ up ⑤ on]

(7)   Do you use a smartphone to look up a word in English that you do not know yet? Or do you look up a word and listen to its pronunciation so you can learn how to say it? Maybe, you might have accessed an application on your phone to help you translate a passage from English to Japanese or Japanese to English. For   5 many years now, intelligent devices have been creeping into the foreign language classroom to assist when students speak with others in a "foreign language". Recently virtual language assistants in the form of small devices, handheld machines, or even robots or "chatbots" are being marketed, sold, and used in   10 many places around the world.

Though these devices are a part of the world of Artificial Intelligence, they are actually based on an application of AI called Machine Learning or ML. ML machines are given enough data or access to the data, and then they teach themselves how to   15 use that data or knowledge. This state-of-the-art technology is based on Arthur Samuel's idea that he contemplated back in 1959. He thought that computers should be taught how to learn for themselves. Using his idea along with the wealth of digitized information on the Internet, engineers began to code machines to   20 think like human beings.

(8)   Machine Learning is advancing so quickly that machines can now read texts and messages and determine the emotion, anger or happiness, behind those messages. When listening to music, these machines can determine what kind of feeling the listener   25 may have when he or she listens to that music. Some devices or

applications can even compose music similar to a particular piece to get a similar feeling from the listeners.

    In the world of language learning, there are now Natural

30 Language Processing (NLP) applications. These applications can help ML devices understand the different feelings and subtle meanings found in the languages used by humans. For example, such devices can use simple English for young children or learners of English to explain a simple process but use more difficult

35 or advanced English for adults or people who have a better understanding of the English language.

    AI devices using ML are now able to teach themselves all the world's languages that have data bases on the Internet. As these devices become increasingly common around the world, the way

40 we use foreign languages will also change. And yes, it is highly possible that one day foreign language teachers may be replaced by AI devices in the classroom. The question remains, will these devices be as funny and multi-talented as many teachers are, or will they just be merely a foreign language teaching machine.

(444 words)

Notes

l. 10   "chatbots" お互いのやり取りを瞬時に外国語に翻訳して話ができるようにした機械
l. 16   state-of-the-art 最新の
l. 17   Arthur Samuel's idea that he contemplated back in 1959
       1959 年には予想されていたアーサーサミュエル (1901-1990 アメリカの計算機科学者)
       の考え
l. 27   a particular piece ある特定の曲
l. 31   subtle meanings found in the languages used by humans
       人間によって使われている言語の中で見られる微妙な意味
l. 40   and yes, そして確かに

1 次の(1)から(5)に続くフレーズとして最も適切なものを下の①から⑤より選びなさい。なお、①から⑤は1回しか使えません。

____ (1) You can learn   ① in many places around the world.

____ (2) Robots are being sold   ② now able to teach themselves.

____ (3) Some devices can   ③ compose music.

____ (4) AI devices are   ④ as funny as many teachers?

____ (5) Will these devices be   ⑤ how to say it.

2 次の(1)から(5)の英文がそれぞれ正しい意味を表すように、和文を参考にして( )に入れる最も適切な語句を下の①から⑩より選びなさい。なお、①から⑩は1回しか使えません。

____ (1) 機械学習の機械は十分なデータを与えられています。

ML machines ( ) enough data.

____ (2) それらは自分自身にそのデータの使い方を教えています。

They teach themselves ( ) use that data.

____ (3) 音楽を聴くと、それらの機械は聞き手が持っているかもしれないどんな種類の感情かを決めることができます。

When ( ) music, these machines can determine what kind of feeling the listener may have.

____ (4) 教室では先生たちが人工知能の道具に置き換わるかもしれません。

Teachers may ( ) by AI devices in the classroom.

____ (5) 私たちの外国語の使い方もまた変わるでしょう。

The way we use foreign languages will also ( ).

① how to	② listen to	③ changed	④ be replaced	⑤ are given
⑥ the way how	⑦ listening to	⑧ change	⑨ replacing	⑩ gave

3 次の(1)から(5)までの英文で本文の内容に合致しているものには ① (= true)を、異なっているものは ② (= false)を書きなさい。

_____ (1) AI is a device that can translate Japanese into English.

_____ (2) In the foreign language classroom, all teachers will become AI machines.

_____ (3) The new AI technology was invented by Arthur Samuel.

_____ (4) AI devices enable us to learn English more effectively.

_____ (5) It is impossible for ML to code foreign languages.

4 〈動詞〉（文には必ず動詞 = Verb が必要となります。動詞が動作や状態を表し、時制や態など文構造や文型を決定する重要な役割を果たします）それぞれの英文の動詞に注意して下線部の空所に適切な日本語を書き入れなさい。

(1) You might have accessed an application on your mobile phone.

みなさんは、携帯電話のアプリに ＿＿＿＿＿＿＿＿＿＿＿＿＿＿ かもしれません。

(2) These devices are actually based on an application of AI called Machine Learning.

これらの装置は実際のところ機械学習と呼ばれる人工知能の応用に ＿＿＿＿＿＿＿＿＿＿

＿＿＿＿＿＿＿＿＿＿ 。

(3) Machine Learning is advancing so quickly that machines can now read texts and messages.

機械学習は急速に ＿＿＿＿＿＿＿＿＿＿ ので機械が今やテキストやメッセージを

＿＿＿＿＿＿＿＿＿＿ ことができます。

(4) As these devices become increasingly common around the world, the way we use foreign languages will also change.

これらの装置が徐々に世界中で普通に ＿＿＿＿＿＿＿＿＿＿ につれて、私たちの外国語の使い方もまた ＿＿＿＿＿＿＿＿＿＿ でしょう。

(5) The question remains.

質問は ＿＿＿＿＿＿＿＿＿＿ 。

Discussion, Paragraph Writing, Presentation

Questions for Discussion

1. When do you use a device (machine) to help you study?
2. Have you ever spoken with a robot or a machine? What did you think?
3. Do you think a robot would make a good teacher? Why? Why not?
4. Some schools no longer allow students to use smart phones, tablets or computers in the classroom. Is this a good idea? Please explain.
5. Describe the first computer you ever used. Ask your teacher to describe their first computer.

Pair Dictation

A 1. My father bought my sister a travel interpreter machine.
   3. Do you have a favorite application for your smart phone?
   5. I replaced my paper dictionary for an electronic version of it.
   7. I spoke in Chinese with a chatbot. It was really interesting.

B 2. My grandmother has never used an electronic dictionary.
   4. My teacher listens to a radio show in French every day.
   6. Language learning is not any easier with an AI device.
   8. My mother uses an AI machine to help her with cooking.

Presentation

Give a short 30 second presentation about your favorite application on your smartphone, tablet, or computer.

I like to use ......

It is a ...... application.

It helps me / I use it to ......

I downloaded it for (free, 200 yen, a subscription rate of ...)

I use it about (1 time, 3 times, for about 1 hour) every day.

I hope you will try it.

Bridges

橋

到達目標

☐ 形容詞について説明できる。

☐ 目的語について説明できる。

☐ 橋とその種類について説明できる。

事前学習 次の単語や熟語を予習して授業を受けましょう。

A 次の(1)から(10)の形容詞（名詞の状態を修飾する品詞で比較の活用をする。名詞を修飾する限定用法と補語になる叙述用法がある）の訳として最も適切な日本語をそれぞれ①から③より、選びなさい。

____ (1) steep 　　　　　[① 険しい 　　② 緩い 　　　③ 遠い 　　　　]
____ (2) wide 　　　　　　[① 狭い 　　　② 高い 　　　③ 広い 　　　　]
____ (3) static 　　　　　[① 動的な 　　② 静的な 　　③ 中ぐらいの]
____ (4) unmoving 　　　[① 静かな 　　② うるさい 　③ 動かない 　]
____ (5) significant 　　[① 重要な 　　② 素晴らしい ③ 簡単な 　　]
____ (6) light 　　　　　[① 軽い 　　　② まぶしい 　③ 右の 　　　　]
____ (7) interesting 　　[① 盛大な 　　② 奇妙な 　　③ 興味深い 　]
____ (8) tensile 　　　　[① 縮んだ 　　② 伸びた 　　③ 緊張した 　]
____ (9) compressive 　[① 圧縮の 　　② 拡大の 　　③ 荘厳な 　　]
____ (10) vertical 　　　[① 垂直の 　　② 水平の 　　③ 斜めの 　　　]

B 次の(1)から(5)の英文に入れる語として最適なものを下の①から⑤より選びなさい。なお、①から⑤は 1 回しか使えません。

____ (1) We should find the environment (　　) which the bridge will be located.

____ (2) Depending (　　) the conditions of the bridge, the beams can either be squeezed or stretched.

____ (3) Beam bridges are bridges made (　　) horizontal beams.

____ (4) Bridges may appear to hang (　　) water.

____ (5) There are other kinds of bridges (　　) well.

[① on 　　② in 　　③ as 　　④ of 　　⑤ over]

(12) Bridges help people cross bodies of waters or steep valleys. When a bridge is being designed, civil engineers, structural engineers, and architects must think about how the bridge will be used, how long and wide it needs to be, and the environment in which the bridge will be located. After answering these questions, 5 the designers must decide the kind of bridge to build.

Bridges are not static or unmoving solid structures. They must adapt to the different weights passing over them as well as to the weather conditions occurring around them. Bridges must be able to react when experiencing a typhoon or an earthquake. 10 Environmental issues are significant for bridges, but more than that, gravity is the issue that designers must consider most. The gravitational forces that affect a bridge are greater when that bridge is big, heavy and long. The shorter and lighter a bridge is, the less the force of gravity affects its structure. 15

(13) To counteract the force of gravity exerted upon a bridge, the forces of compression and tension must be carefully balanced. Compression is the force that pushes inward, while tension is a force that stretches and pulls outward. The weight of the bridge's structure as well as its load must be channeled onto the supports 20 at the bridge's ends and onto the piers underneath its span. Each type of bridge has its own particular way of balancing these forces while supporting the weight of the bridge and its load.

Beam bridges are bridges made of horizontal beams supported by piers at each end of the bridge. The piers are always in a 25 state of compression. Depending on the conditions of the bridge, the beams can either be squeezed or stretched. In other words, they experience both tension and compression.

Arch bridges are easily recognized for their arched shape.
30 These bridges support their loads by distributing the compressive forces both across the arch and down it. An interesting characteristic of an arch is that it is always pushing in on itself.

(14)   A suspension bridge is a bridge that may appear to hang over water or in mid-air. The towers of this type of bridge are always
35 in a state of compression. The deck area of a suspension bridge hangs from sturdy cables that are in a state of tension; the deck must be able to experience both tension and compression.

A truss bridge has a beam structure with reinforcements. The deck of a truss bridge is in tension. The trusses must be able to
40 withstand both tensile and compressive forces. Diagonal trusses are in a state of tension, while vertical ones are in a state of compression.

There are other kinds of bridges as well. Some are very unique and beautiful. But the most important aspect of a bridge is how
45 it connects people and places together.

(471words)

Notes

l. 8	adapt to 適合する
l. 10	react (to) （に）反応する
l. 16	counteract 逆らう
l. 16	gravity exerted upon a bridge 橋にかかる重力
l. 17	compression 圧縮
l. 17	tension 張力
l. 20	load 負荷
l. 21	pier 橋脚
l. 21	span 梁間、支間（支柱と支柱の間の間隔）
l. 24	beam bridge 桁橋
l. 29	arch bridge アーチ橋
l. 33	suspension bridge つり橋
l. 35	deck 橋の床
l. 38	truss bridge トラス橋

1 次の(1)から(5)に続くフレーズとして最も適切なものを下の①から⑤より選びなさい。なお、①から⑤は 1 回しか使えません。

____ (1) Bridges help

____ (2) Bridges are not

____ (3) Compression is the force

____ (4) These bridges support their loads

____ (5) A truss bridge has a

① static solid structures.

② that pushes inward.

③ people cross bodies of waters.

④ by distributing the compressive forces.

⑤ beam structure with reinforcements.

2 次の(1)から(5)の英文がそれぞれ正しい意味を表すように、和文を参考にして ( ) に入れる最も適切な語を下の①から⑩より選びなさい。なお、①から⑩は 1 回しか使えません。

____ (1) 建築家は橋がどのように使われるかを考えなくてはいけません。

Architects must think about ( ) the bridge will be used.

____ (2) 環境の問題は橋にとっては重要です。

Environmental ( ) are significant for bridges.

____ (3) 橋脚はいつも圧力のかかっている状態にあります。

The piers are always in a ( ) of compression.

____ (4) トラスは張力にも圧力にも耐えることができなくてはいけません。

The trusses must be able to ( ) both tensile and compressive forces.

____ (5) 橋の中には、個性的で美しいものもあるでしょう。

Some are very ( ) and beautiful.

① what	② issue	③ state	④ supported	⑤ issues
⑥ withstand	⑦ site	⑧ ensure	⑨ unique	⑩ how

3　次の(1)から(5)までの英文で本文の内容に合致しているものには ① (= true)を、異なっているものは ② (= false)を書きなさい。

____ (1)　Some bridges are very difficult for us to cross.

____ (2)　When designing bridges, the architects need to think about structural problems.

____ (3)　Beam bridges are supported by the force of arch structures.

____ (4)　A suspension bridge has a beam structure with reinforcements.

____ (5)　The deck of a bridge is the space to cross it.

4　〈目的語〉（目的語 = Object は動詞の対象のことです。目的語は名詞、名詞句、名詞節が担います。）それぞれの英文の目的語に注意して下線部の空所に適切な日本語を書き入れなさい。

(1)　The designers must decide the kind of bridge to build.

設計者は、_____を決めなくてはいけません。

(2)　Each type of bridge has its own particular way of balancing these forces.

それぞれの橋の種類には、_____があります。

(3)　These bridges support their loads by distributing the compressive forces both across the arch and down it.

これらの橋はアーチの上と下の両方の圧力を分けることによって_____を支えています。

(4)　A truss bridge has a beam structure with reinforcements.

トラス橋は、_____を持っています。

(5)　The deck must be able to experience both tension and compression.

橋の床面は_____の両方に対応していなくてはいけません。

Discussion, Paragraph Writing, Presentation

Questions for Discussion

1. What is your favorite kind of bridge? Why? Can you describe it?
2. Name your favorite bridge in Japan (or the world). What kind of bridge is it? Describe it for your group.
   I like ... It looks like a .... It is made of (steel, concrete, wood, brick). It is ... long and ... wide.
   It is for (trains, cars, bicycles, people ......) It was made in ......
3. Have you ever walked across a rope or simple wooden bridge? How did you feel at that time?
4. There are many kinds of bridges. Can you name a few and describe them?
5. Do you like to cross over bridges or pass through tunnels? Why?

Pair Dictation

15 **A** 1. The Golden Gate Bridge is a suspension bridge.
   3. The Danyang-Kunshan Grand Bridge in China is the longest bridge in the world.
   5. The truck is too heavy to cross this bridge.
   7. This bridge was made 300 years ago.

16 **B** 2. London Bridge is a bridge made of concrete and steel.
   4. The Eshima-Ohashi Bridge is one of the steepest bridges in the world.
   6. Only one person at a time can walk across this rope bridge.
   8. The longest bridge in the world is over 160 kilometers long.

Presentation

Describe the photo below.

What do you think the people are looking at?

What do you think the people on the top are talking about?

Would you like to be at the top of this bridge, or the bottom? Why?

Games

ゲーム

到達目標

□ 副詞について説明できる。

□ 補語について説明できる。

□ ゲームの開発に必要なことについて説明できる。

事前学習 次の単語や熟語を予習して授業を受けましょう。

A 次の(1)から(10)の副詞(動詞、形容詞などを修飾する品詞で文全体、副詞自体を修飾することもある。)の訳として最も適切な日本語をそれぞれ①から③より、選びなさい。

____	(1)	increasingly	[① ますます	② しばしば	③ 急激に	]
____	(2)	once	[① 過去	② ひとたび	③ 何度も	]
____	(3)	recently	[① 最後に	② 最近では	③ 頻繁に	]
____	(4)	therefore	[① なぜなら	② それゆえに	③ そこでは	]
____	(5)	furthermore	[① なおその上に	② しかしながら	③ その結果	]
____	(6)	primarily	[① 主として	② 高く	③ ゆっくりと	]
____	(7)	ultimately	[① 最初に	② 最終的には	③ 絶対に	]
____	(8)	truly	[① 本当に	② まっすぐに	③ 早く	]
____	(9)	quite	[① 全く	② ちょうど	③ 静かに	]
____	(10)	today	[① 今の	② 今日では	③ こんにちは	]

B 次の(1)から(5)の英文に入れる語として最適なものを下の①から⑤より選びなさい。なお、①から⑤は1回しか使えません。

____ (1) Some games are based (　　) a movie.

____ (2) Do you like (　　) play games?

____ (3) 2D graphics are incorporated (　　) many games.

____ (4) Programming skills in both C (　　) other languages are necessary.

____ (5) Math skills as (　　) as programming skills are necessary too.

[① well 　② and 　③ upon 　④ to 　⑤ into]

(17)   Do you like to play cards? Board games? Computerized or
video games? Games on your smartphone or a small hand-
held device? Games are a very popular form of entertainment
and increasingly electronic games are becoming one of the most
popular forms of recreation and entertainment around the world.   5

When electronic and computerized games first appeared,
the games were quite simple. The first computerized game
was based on the simple game of table tennis, a sport that
many people enjoy world-wide. After that, software engineers,
computer engineers, and electrical engineers began writing   10
programs that had little bugs moving across screens while eating
dots of candy, or that had space ships flying through space while
doing battle with other ships.

(18)   Today creating a game is not the work of just one person or
even a small team of engineers. It takes many kinds of engineers   15
to make a game. Some games are based upon a movie, a comic
book or maybe a short story; other games might be based upon
a script devised by a creative group formed for just that purpose.
Once the game or story-line is determined, game engine
programmers begin to create the basic engine of the game.   20

Another type of engineer necessary to create a game is a
graphics engine programmer. The graphics used for video
games are now primarily 3D graphics. To create these graphics,
programmers must have a good understanding of vector and
matrix mathematics as well as quaternions and linear algebra.   25

Recently, as a growing number of people play games on their smartphones, 2D graphics are again being incorporated into many games. Some games have background music and sound effects to accompany them; therefore, sound programmers are also

30 necessary to help create a game.

(19) Furthermore, programmers must also determine how players will access the game. Will it be from a game console or via the Internet? Will it be from a smartphone or a small hand-held gaming device? Will it be for only one player or for many players

35 or teams? And will the players use their fingers, a mouse, a joy stick or their keyboard to play the game?

Making a good game requires so many different types of skills. Advanced math skills as well as coding and programming skills in both C and other languages are all necessary. Excellent graphics,

40 great sound and sound effects are also vital. But to make the game truly a success, the story behind the game and the way that the game is played and ultimately won are what will make it a winner among gamers the world over.

(432 words)

Notes

l. 24　vector and matrix mathematics　ベクトルと行列数学
l. 25　quaternions and linear algebra　四元数と線形数学
l. 39　C (language)　C言語＝プログラム言語の一種
l. 40　vital　必須の

Exercises

1 次の(1)から(5)に続くフレーズとして最も適切なものを下の①から⑤より選びなさい。なお、①から⑤は1回しか使えません。

____ (1) Games are a very popular

____ (2) Creating a game is not

____ (3) Programmers must determine

____ (4) Making a good game

____ (5) Some games have

① the work of just one person.

② requires many different types of skills.

③ background music and sound effects.

④ form of entertainment.

⑤ how players will access the game.

2 次の(1)から(5)の英文がそれぞれ正しい意味を表すように、和文を参考にして( )に入れる最も適切な語を下の①から⑩より選びなさい。なお、①から⑩は1回しか使えません。

____ (1) 最初のコンピュータゲームは単純な卓球のゲームに基づいていました。

The first computerized game was ( ) on the simple game of table tennis.

____ (2) ビデオゲームに使われるグラフィックスは3次元グラフィックスです。

The graphics ( ) for video games are 3D graphics.

____ (3) 音響効果もまた必須です。

Sound effects are also ( ).

____ (4) ゲームにはそれに伴うバックグランウドミュージックや音響効果もあります。

Some games have background music and sound effects to ( ) them.

____ (5) ゲームへのアクセスの仕方はスマホからでしょうか、それとも小さな携帯用のゲーム機器からでしょうか。

Will it ( ) from a smartphone or a small hand-held gaming device?

① vital	② using	③ base	④ visual	⑤ took
⑥ based	⑦ be	⑧ used	⑨ accompany	⑩ being

3 次の(1)から(5)までの英文で本文の内容に合致しているものには ① (= true)を、異なっているものは ② (= false)を書きなさい。

___ (1) Video games are mainly on the Internet.

___ (2) The first computerized game was based on a world-wide sport.

___ (3) Programming games needs knowledge of math.

___ (4) All games must have sound effects and original stories.

___ (5) The most important thing to make a game popular is the story behind the game.

4 〈補語〉（補語 = <u>C</u>omplement は前に置かれている名詞の意味内容を補助する語のことです。名詞や形容詞が担います。）それぞれの英文の補語に注意して下線部の空所に適切な日本語を書き入れなさい。

(1) Electronic games are becoming one of the most popular forms of recreation.

電子ゲームは、＿＿＿＿＿＿＿＿＿＿＿＿＿＿＿＿＿＿＿＿＿になってきています。

(2) The first games were quite simple.

最初のゲームは、とても＿＿＿＿＿＿＿＿＿＿＿＿＿＿＿＿＿でした。

(3) Sound programmers are also necessary to help create a game.

音声のプログラマーもまたゲームの製作には＿＿＿＿＿＿＿＿＿＿＿＿＿＿＿です。

(4) Advanced math skills are all necessary.

応用数学の技能はみな、＿＿＿＿＿＿＿＿＿＿＿＿＿＿＿＿＿です。

(5) The story behind the game is what will make it a winner.

ゲームの背後にある物語こそがゲームを＿＿＿＿＿＿＿＿＿＿＿にするものなのです。

Discussion, Paragraph Writing, Presentation

Questions for Discussion

1. Which do you like better, board games, card games, or computer games? Why?
2. What is your favorite game to play? When do you play it?
3. What was your favorite game to play when you were an elementary student?
4. How much time do you spend in a day playing games? (in a day, on Saturday / Sunday, in a week)
5. Where do you like to play games? Who do you like to play games with?
6. What is a game that is fun to play but would not be good on a computer?

Pair Work Dictation

A
1. My brother plays games every night for 30 minutes before he takes a bath.
3. I like action games, but my mother likes puzzle games.
5. My parents sometimes let me play their old family computer games.
7. I love the graphics for this game. They are so beautiful.

B
2. I don't like to play electronic games, but I like to play cards.
4. Our university has an esports team.
6. Making sound effects for a game is really difficult.
8. I finally won a game of Shogi against the computer.

Pair presentation

Give a pair presentation on a Japanese traditional game or a board game you know. (1 to 2 minute presentation)

1. One person should describe the game.
2. One person should explain the rules and how to win.

Physics of Jet Coasters

ジェットコースターの物理学

到達目標

□ 修飾（形容詞＋名詞）について説明できる。

□ ジェットコースターの仕組みについて説明できる。

□ エネルギーの種類について説明できる。

事前学習　次の単語を予習して授業を受けましょう。

A　次の(1)から(10)の英語の訳として最も適切な日本語をそれぞれ①から③より、選びなさい。

____ (1) amusement [① 驚き ② 娯楽 ③ 前菜]
____ (2) scream [① 叫ぶ ② 凍らす ③ 夢を見る]
____ (3) fascinate [① 熱中する ② 飽きる ③ 通う]
____ (4) dynamic [① 動的な ② 静かな ③ 劇的な]
____ (5) potential [① 潜在的な ② 可能性のある ③ 静止]
____ (6) factor [① 必要 ② 要因 ③ 結果]
____ (7) gravity [① 引力 ② 慣性 ③ 絶対に]
____ (8) kinetic [① 運動の ② 熱の ③ 火力の]
____ (9) friction [① 摩擦 ② 引火 ③ 消しゴム]
____ (10) descent [① 上昇 ② 下降 ③ 丁寧な]

B　次の(1)から(5)の日本語の訳として最も適切な英語をそれぞれ①から③より、選びなさい。

____ (1) 固定した [① fixed ② connected ③ landscape]
____ (2) 喜ばせる [① entertain ② attract ③ happen]
____ (3) 高く上がる [① high ② height ③ soar]
____ (4) 飛び込む [① drive ② dive ③ die]
____ (5) 進化する [① evolve ② exclude ③ erupt]

(22) Amusement parks are places where people love to laugh, scream, spin, soar and dive. Upside down, right-side up, spinning up and down and to the left and the right are all part of some of the attractions and rides at amusement parks.

The first fixed amusement park was built for the Columbian   5
Exposition held in the United States in Chicago. In 1893 a midway area was built for people to enjoy games and rides. The first Ferris Wheel was built for this area. From that time on, engineers have continued to build amusement parks around the world to amuse and entertain people with new and exciting experiences.   10

(23) Many visitors to an amusement park are fascinated by the landscape or the theme of the park while others are attracted immediately to the fast and dynamic rides. Most people only think about the thrill of the speed and height of a ride, but engineers look at each ride differently. For a roller coaster,   15
engineers must consider both potential energy and kinetic energy and how these two types of energy work together to make a ride not only exciting but also safe.

Potential energy is the energy used to pull a car up a steep hill or incline. Usually this energy comes from a motorized source.   20
Once the car has achieved its highest height, then the potential energy no longer is a factor, and the motor is no longer connected to the car. At that point, gravity and kinetic energy take over. The car will begin its quick descent along a track of twists, turns

25 and possibly even 360 degree loops before the car comes to a complete and safe stop.

(24) Calculations of the potential energy and the kinetic energy must be accurate. If the car is making a 360 degree loop and there is not enough kinetic energy, the car will fall off the tracks before it
30 reaches the top of the loop and it won't be able to complete the circle. Engineers must make certain that the peaks of the loops are lower than the initial starting point of the car.

Engineers must also consider friction when they design a roller coaster. Friction happens when a car moves over the tracks.
35 If there is too much friction, then the car will not have enough kinetic energy or speed to complete the ride. So the weight of the car and passengers must all be considered when determining the necessary potential energy and kinetic energy.

Amusement parks have evolved over time from a simple swing
40 or peaceful Ferris Wheel to small jets propelled on tracks. Roller coasters are both thrilling to ride and challenging to make.

(447 words)

Notes

l. 8   Ferris Wheel   観覧車
l. 23   take over   引き継ぐ

Exercises

1 次の(1)から(5)に続くフレーズとして最も適切なものを下の①から⑤より選びなさい。なお、①から⑤は1回しか使えません。

_____ (1) Amusements parks are places

_____ (2) Many visitors to an amusement park are

_____ (3) Potential energy is the

_____ (4) Engineers must make certain that

_____ (5) Engineers must also consider friction

① fascinated by the landscape.

② energy used to pull a car up a steep hill.

③ when they design a roller coaster.

④ the 360 degree loop's highest point is lower than the initial starting point.

⑤ where people love to laugh.

2 次の(1)から(5)の英文がそれぞれ正しい意味を表すように、和文を参考にして( )に入れる最も適切な語を下の①から⑩より選びなさい。なお、①から⑩は1回しか使えません。

_____ (1) 最初の観覧車はこの地域に作られました。

The ( ) Ferris Wheel was built for this area.

_____ (2) 彼らは人々をワクワクするような経験で喜ばせたがっていました。

They wanted to entertain people with ( ) experiences.

_____ (3) このエネルギーはエンジンのついた動力から来ています。

This energy comes from a ( ) source.

_____ (4) 車は安全に止まります。

The car comes to a ( ) stop.

_____ (5) 十分な運動エネルギーがありません。

There is not ( ) kinetic energy.

| ① safety | ② exciting | ③ first | ④ one | ⑤ enough |
| ⑥ excited | ⑦ each | ⑧ safe | ⑨ monitoring | ⑩ motorized |

3 次の(1)から(5)までの英文で本文の内容に合致しているものには ① (= true)を、異なっているものは ② (= false)を書きなさい。

____ (1) It was dangerous for people to ride the first Ferris Wheel.

____ (2) Engineers have to calculate friction when constructing the Ferris Wheel in an amusement park.

____ (3) Potential energy is the energy used to complete the ride.

____ (4) Constructing an amusement park needs the knowledge of energy.

____ (5) It is important to entertain people with a jet coaster.

4 〈修飾関係〉(形容詞は名詞の前や後ろについて名詞を修飾します。大きな名詞句、名詞節として文中で主語や目的語の役割を果たします。)それぞれの英文の修飾関係に注意して下線部の空所に適切な日本語を書き入れなさい。

(1) Engineers have continued to build amusement parks around the world.

技術者たちは世界中に＿＿＿＿＿＿＿＿＿＿＿＿＿を作り続けています。

(2) Others are attracted to the fast and dynamic rides.

他の人たちも、＿＿＿＿＿＿＿＿＿＿＿な乗り物にひきつけられます。

(3) If there is too much friction, then the car will not have enough kinetic energy.

もし、あまりに摩擦が大きいと、車は＿＿＿＿＿＿＿＿＿な運動エネルギーを持てなくなるでしょう。

(4) Amusement parks have evolved from a simple swing.

遊園地は、＿＿＿＿＿＿＿＿＿＿＿なブランコから進化してきています。

(5) The energy will pull a car up a steep hill.

そのエネルギーが、車を＿＿＿＿＿＿＿＿＿＿＿な丘に引き上げるのです。

Discussion, Paragraph Writing, Presentation

Questions for Discussion

1. What makes a ride spectacular? Exciting?
2. What is the most important part of an amusement park?
3. Do you like virtual (3D / 4D) rides or real rides?
4. What is a ride you would like to ride over and over again? Why?
5. What is more exciting, waiting for the ride or riding the ride?

Pair Dictation

A
1. My family goes to an amusement park every year for my dad's birthday.
3. My friend is a graphic engineer working at an amusement park in Kyushu.
5. Gravity and kinetic energy help cars on roller coasters go fast.
7. Everyone screamed when the roller coaster went down the hill.

B
2. I like to ride wooden roller coasters.
4. Most people waiting in line for the ride were talking with their friends.
6. Potential energy helps a car go up an incline on a roller coaster.
8. Many children love the airplane ride that goes up and down and around and around.

Summary Practice: Complete this summary of the passage.

The first fixed amusement park (   ). Since then,
engineers have continued to build (   ) and
(   ). (   ) are popular rides. These
rides use both (   ). Potential energy
helps (   ). (   )
move the car through the twists, loops and turns. (   ) is another
factor engineers consider (   ).

What are the key words in this passage?

Who?   What?   Where?

**After completing this, please practice reading aloud with your partner.

Smart Cities

スマートシティ

到達目標
- □ 後置修飾（分詞と関係詞）について説明できる。
- □ スマートシティの特徴について説明できる。

事前学習 次の単語を予習して授業を受けましょう。

A 次の(1)から(10)の英語の訳として最も適切な日本語をそれぞれ①から③より、選びなさい。

____	(1)	smart	[	① 賢い	② やせた	③ 細い	]
____	(2)	equipment	[	① 装置	② 道具	③ 方向	]
____	(3)	reside	[	① 追いやる	② 捨てる	③ 居住する	]
____	(4)	prevent	[	① 促す	② 証明する	③ 妨げる	]
____	(5)	resource	[	① 源	② 資料	③ 資産	]
____	(6)	notice	[	① 気づく	② 経過する	③ 目立つ	]
____	(7)	garbage	[	① 開発	② ごみ	③ 処理場	]
____	(8)	renewable	[	① 最新の	② 再生可能な	③ 置き換え可能な	]
____	(9)	destination	[	① 目的	② 目的地	③ 運命	]
____	(10)	disseminate	[	① 拡散させる	② 収束する	③ 指示する	]

B 次の(1)から(5)の日本語の訳として最も適切な英語をそれぞれ①から③より、選びなさい。

____	(1)	都市部の	[	① rural	② urban	③ setting	]
____	(2)	保存する	[	① conclude	② construct	③ conserve	]
____	(3)	市民	[	① civil	② citizen	③ city	]
____	(4)	分類する	[	① sort	② sell	③ sink	]
____	(5)	収集する	[	① collect	② correct	③ conclude	]

Reading

(27)   Just a few years ago, the word "smart" was used mostly to describe an intelligent person. But recently, with the evolution of mobile phones from mere communication devices into equipment which are practically small hand-held computers, "smart" now is most commonly associated with something that is operated using   5 a computer. So, now we have smart phones, cars, homes and even cities.

Today, over 50% of the world's population lives in an urban setting or a city; in 10 years, more than 60% will reside in cities. Water and energy usage, pollution, as well as housing   10 and transportation problems are some of the issues that all cities must try to solve. One way of doing that is to become a "smart" city - a city that uses smart technologies and data as a means to solve its sustainability challenges.

(28)   Information and communication technology are used   15 throughout the city to solve various problems and to help prevent other problems as well. For example, collected weather data can help citizens know when it is a good time to water their gardens. Such information can help a city to conserve its water resources.

The new city of Songdo, Korea, is an urban area that has been   20 built with smart technology at its core. Driving through the city, one will notice that there are no garbage bins or trash collection trucks. The trash from each home is sucked down into a system under the city. From there the city's garbage goes to processing centers where it is automatically sorted for recycling and then   25 processed. This process is not only environmentally friendly, but also uses some of the waste to help generate renewable energy.

(29)   Likewise, cities that are smart can provide data to drivers throughout the area. With up-to-date information, drivers can
30 avoid traffic jams and reach their destinations more quickly. As almost 40% of traffic in the central metropolitan areas is caused by drivers searching for places to park their cars, information collected from a smart city network could help those drivers find parking lots or spaces more effectively.

35   With cameras and other data collection devices placed throughout urban areas, crimes may now be solved more easily or perhaps even prevented. Collecting, analyzing and disseminating data gathered every second in a city will become increasingly important in the future. Moreover, protecting that data and using
40 it for the citizens' best interests will become equally important. Smart cities are here to stay, and we too must be smart in how we live and work in these new, smart, urban environments.

(424 words)

Notes

l. 14   sustainability challenges   持続可能な取り組み
l. 23   be sucked down   飲み込まれる
l. 31   the central metropolitan area   中心の大都会の地域

Exercises

1 次の(1)から(5)に続くフレーズとして最も適切なものを下の①から⑤より選びなさい。なお、①から⑤は1回しか使えません。

____ (1) Over 50% of the world's population lives

____ (2) Data can help us know

____ (3) The city's garbage goes

____ (4) Traffic jams are caused

____ (5) Smart cities are

① here to stay.

② when it is a good time to water our gardens.

③ by drivers searching for places to park their cars.

④ to processing centers.

⑤ in an urban setting or a city.

2 次の(1)から(5)の英文がそれぞれ正しい意味を表すように、和文を参考にして( )に入れる最も適切な語句を下の①から⓪より選びなさい。なお、①から⑩は1回しか使えません。

____ (1) 「スマート」という語は何かコンピュータを使って操作されることと関連しています。
The word "smart" is associated with something ( ) is operated using a computer.

____ (2) 街のごみは、自動的にリサイクル用に分類される処理センターに向かいます。
The city's garbage goes to processing centers ( ) it is automatically sorted for recycling.

____ (3) スマートシティのネットワークから集められた情報によって、ドライバーは駐車場を見つけられるでしょう。
Information ( ) from a smart city network could help those drivers find parking lots.

____ (4) 都市部中に置かれたカメラによって、犯罪は防がれるかもしれません。
With cameras ( ) throughout urban areas, crimes may be prevented.

____ (5) スマートな都市はその地域にいるドライバーにデータを供給します。
Cities that ( ) smart can provide data to drivers throughout the area.

| ① this | ② when | ③ where | ④ are | ⑤ is |
| ⑥ those | ⑦ placed | ⑧ given | ⑨ collected | ⑩ that |

3 次の(1)から(5)までの英文で本文の内容に合致しているものには ① (= true)を、異なっているものは ② (= false)を書きなさい。

_____ (1) Many intelligent people are living in smart cities.

_____ (2) The word "smart" means something operated by computers.

_____ (3) In smart cities, it is easy to treat garbage in clean ways.

_____ (4) Many people are using smart phones, but they haven't noticed the smart phone's usefulness.

_____ (5) When collecting data from a city, it is important to protect and use the data.

4 〈修飾関係〉（後置修飾とは、名詞の後ろに分詞や関係詞節がついて前の名詞（= 先行詞）を修飾します。修飾される名詞の後で形容詞句、形容詞節の役割を果たします。）それぞれの英文の修飾関係に注意して下線部の空所に適切な日本語を書き入れなさい。

(1) Mobile phones are changed from mere communication devices into equipment which are practically small hand-held computers.

携帯電話は、単なるコミュニケーションの道具から＿＿＿＿＿＿＿＿＿＿＿＿＿＿＿＿＿＿の装置に変化しています。

(2) Collecting, analyzing and disseminating data gathered in a city will become important in the future.

都市で＿＿＿＿＿＿＿＿＿＿＿＿＿＿＿データの集約、分析、拡散させることは将来重要になるでしょう。

(3) Environmental problems are some of the issues that all cities must try to solve.

環境の問題は、＿＿＿＿＿＿＿＿＿＿＿＿＿＿＿＿＿問題のいくつかです。

(4) Moreover, protecting that data and using it for the citizens' best interests will become important.

さらには、市民の最大の利益のために＿＿＿＿＿＿＿＿＿＿＿＿＿＿は重要になるでしょう。

(5) The new city is an urban area that has been built with smart technology at its core.

その新しい都市は、中核部にスマートテクノロジーを備えて＿＿＿＿＿＿＿＿＿＿＿＿＿都市部なのです。

Discussion, Paragraph Writing, Presentation

Discussion Questions:

1. Is your community a "smart" community?   If yes, how is it "smart"? If "no", do you want your community to become a "smart" one?
2. How do you think a "smart" city can help make our lives better?
3. Would you like your school to be a "smart" school? If your school was smart, how would your school life be different?
4. Do you think "smart" cities can help prevent crimes and trouble in our lives?
5. Are "smart" cities and all the data collected in them "safe"?

Pair Practice

(30) **A** 1. I have lived in my community all my life.
   3. The new factory has smart features installed throughout the area.
   5. Since we moved into a smart home, our energy bill has dropped.
   7. My community has strict rules about recycling plastic bottles and paper.

(31) **B** 2. My cousins live in a rural area, so it takes them 1 hour to get to school.
   4. This new GPS helps me find a good parking place in downtown Tokyo.
   6. Analyzing data is difficult when there is a large amount of data collected every day.
   8. I can send my camera's data to my computer when I press this button.

Summary Writing: Complete this summary of the passage

"Smart" is a word (   ). A "smart" city is
(   ) that uses (   ) to help be
sustainable. Smart cities use data to help (   ).
(   ) data gathered in cities will become more
and more important. Protecting the data will (   ).

**After completing this summary, please read it aloud 3 times.

Tokyo Skytree

東京スカイツリー

到達目標
☐ 内容に沿って要点をまとめることができる。
☐ 東京スカイツリーの特徴について説明できる。

事前学習 次の単語を予習して授業を受けましょう。

A 次の(1)から(10)の英語の訳として最も適切な日本語をそれぞれ①から③より、選びなさい。

____ (1) structure [① 方向 ② 構造 ③ 基礎]
____ (2) correct [① 正しい ② 集める ③ 不正の]
____ (3) participate [① 分ける ② 投げる ③ 参加する]
____ (4) transmit [① 送る ② 翻訳する ③ 構築する]
____ (5) equilateral [① 等辺の ② 等角の ③ 相似の]
____ (6) triangle [① 長方形 ② 正方形 ③ 三角形]
____ (7) reinforced [① 強化した ② 雨天の ③ 回転した]
____ (8) circular [① 三角の ② 四角の ③ 丸い]
____ (9) pagoda [① 尖塔 ② 仏塔 ③ 聖地]
____ (10) stable [① 不安定な ② 安定した ③ 固定した]

B 次の(1)から(5)の日本語の訳として最も適切な英語をそれぞれ①から③より、選びなさい。

____ (1) 放送 [① broadcast ② radioactive ③ digital]
____ (2) 貢献する [① contribute ② construct ③ conclude]
____ (3) 地震 [① confidence ② tradition ③ earthquake]
____ (4) 直径 [① centimeter ② diameter ③ base]
____ (5) 連結する [① combine ② connection ③ concrete]

(32) Do you know what the tallest structure in Japan is? If you answered "Tokyo Skytree", you are correct!

More than 100 architects, engineers, and planners participated in the planning, designing and building of this tower. The tower transmits radio waves for broadcasting digital television and radio   5 programs across Japan.

There are three main ideas behind the design of Tokyo Skytree. The first idea is to combine a future design with Japan's traditional beauty. The second idea is to help revitalize the city. The third idea is to contribute to disaster prevention in Japan.   10

(33) The base of the structure is an equilateral triangle. There are three sides to the base, and each side is as long as the other sides. They are all 68 meters long. Just like any tall strong tree, Tokyo Skytree has strong and deep roots. Reinforced steel and concrete make the base. This foundation base is not as long as   15 a soccer field, but it is half the length of one. It goes 50 meters down into the ground. Tokyo Skytree has high-strength steel tubes at the base of the tower. These tubes are 2.3 meters in diameter and the thickness of each tube is 10 centimeters. As the structure gets higher, the triangle shape changes into a   20 circular shape. This change helps the structure stay stable.

While architects helped to make the design of Tokyo Skytree appear to be both futuristic and traditional, engineers helped to make the structure sound and safe in a strong earthquake. When

25 designing the structure, engineers also considered strong winds higher than 70 to 80 meters per second. Traditional engineering similar to that found in pagodas in Japanese temples was used along with high-tech engineering to make this structure safe and sound.

(34)   Visitors to Tokyo Skytree can go up to two observation decks. The first observation deck is at 350 meters. This deck is taller than the Tokyo Tower, and 2000 people can visit this deck at one time. The second deck is at 450 meters, and 900 people can visit this deck at one time. It takes about 30 seconds by elevator to go
35 from the base of the structure to the first observation area, and it takes a little less than a minute to go to the second observation deck. Tokyo Skytree will definitely be a place for many people to visit for years to come.

(404 words)

Exercises

1 次の(1)から(5)に続くフレーズとして最も適切なものを下の①から⑤より選びなさい。なお、①から⑤は1回しか使えません。

____ (1) Visitors to Tokyo Skytree

____ (2) It takes about 30 seconds by elevator

____ (3) Tokyo Skytree is a place

____ (4) It goes 50 meters

____ (5) The base of the structure is

① down into the ground.

② to go to the first observation area.

③ an equilateral triangle.

④ can go up to two observation decks.

⑤ for many people to visit.

2 次の(1)から(5)の英文がそれぞれ正しい意味を表すように、和文を参考にして( )に入れる最も適切な語句を下の①から⑩より選びなさい。なお、①から⑩は1回しか使えません。

____ (1) 最初の展望台は350メートルのところにあります。

The first observation deck is ( ) 350 meters.

____ (2) この展望台は東京タワーより高いです。

This deck is ( ) than the Tokyo Tower.

____ (3) 2番目の展望台に行くには一分もかかりません。

It takes a little ( ) than a minute to go to the second observation deck.

____ (4) 伝統的な技術は日本の寺院建築である仏塔にみられるものと似ています。

Traditional engineering is similar ( ) that found in pagodas in Japanese temples.

____ (5) この変化は構造体を安定させるのに役立ちます。

This change helps the structure ( ) stable.

| ① in | ② tallest | ③ less | ④ to | ⑤ stay |
| ⑥ at | ⑦ taller | ⑧ least | ⑨ for | ⑩ sit |

3 本文の内容について下記の設問に日本語で答えなさい。

(1) 日本で一番高い建物である東京スカイツリーは何のための建物ですか。

_____

(2) 東京スカイツリーの設計の３つの意図について説明しなさい。

① _____

② _____

③ _____

(3) 東京スカイツリーの構造についてまとめなさい。

基礎（土台）の構造 _____

_____

鋼管の大きさと構造 _____

_____

耐震と強風について _____

_____

(4) 東京スカイツリーの展望台について説明しなさい。

The first deck _____

_____

The second deck _____

_____

Discussion, Paragraph Writing, Presentation

Questions for discussion:

1. How can Tokyo Skytree help bring life to Tokyo?
2. What is the tallest tower or look-out point in your area? Have you visited there? What can you see?
3. Have you ever seen a pagoda in Japan? Where did you see it? Could you go inside?
4. In what ways is Tokyo Skytree used for disaster prevention?
5. Have you visited Tokyo Skytree? If so, what did you think? If not, would you like to go?

Pair Practice

(35) **A**
1. The swimming pool is for short races, so it is only 25 meters long.
3. The foundation of this building goes 50 meters down from sea level.
5. The walls in this building are very thick and soundproof.
7. I love to visit the observation deck at the airport and watch the airplanes take off.

(36) **B**
2. This building is 45 stories high and has an observation deck on the top floor.
4. That high-rise circular building is the apartment building where I live.
6. The tallest building in my community is only 20 stories high.
8. I am afraid of heights, so I don't like to go up into skyscrapers.

Presentation Skills

Give a 1 minute presentation on your favorite landmark or sightseeing place in your community.

Sportswear and Technology

スポーツウェアとテクノロジー

到達目標

□ 内容に沿って、因果関係などをまとめることが
できる。

□ スポーツとテクノロジーの関係について説明で
きる。

事前学習 次の単語を予習して授業を受けましょう。

A 次の(1)から(10)の英語の訳として最も適切な日本語をそれぞれ①から③より、選びなさい。

____ (1) athlete [① 呼吸 ② 運動選手 ③ 競技場]

____ (2) gather [① 集合する ② 壊す ③ 離れる]

____ (3) arena [① 闘牛場 ② プール ③ 陸上競技場]

____ (4) monitor [① 展示する ② 観察する ③ 検査する]

____ (5) pulse [① 血圧 ② 脈拍 ③ 血糖値]

____ (6) respiratory [① 呼吸の ② 想像の ③ 怪我の]

____ (7) affix [① 添える ② 切り分ける ③ 取り上げる]

____ (8) official [① 審判 ② 事務室 ③ 用意]

____ (9) absorb [① 吸う ② 吐く ③ 固める]

____ (10) posture [① 姿勢 ② ポスター ③ 展示物]

B 次の(1)から(5)の日本語の訳として最も適切な英語をそれぞれ①から③より、選びなさい。

____ (1) 数えきれない [① countless ② counter ③ limited]

____ (2) コーチ [① coach ② caught ③ expert]

____ (3) 支持者 [① offer ② sponsor ③ trainer]

____ (4) 進化 [① adventure ② advance ③ advertisement]

____ (5) 汗 [① sweat ② urine ③ injury]

Reading

(37) Do you like sports? Are they something you like to do or something you like to watch? Many people like to do both, and this is especially true every four years when the world's athletes gather for the Olympic Games. Before even stepping into the world arena, athletes spend countless hours training and ₅ perfecting their sport. Many of these athletes have a large group of coaches, trainers, medical experts and technology engineers as well as financial sponsors to assist them in their quest to become the best in their sport.

Hard work and training are crucial for every athlete, but ₁₀ these days it requires more than that to be successful. Today coaches and trainers collect data from the training records and performances of athletes, and they carefully monitor the athletes during their training sessions. Years ago, coaches and trainers would monitor athletes by visual observation, a stopwatch and ₁₅ perhaps a quick pulse and respiratory check after each training session. Now, they spend much more time looking at their computers while an athlete is training.

(38) One reason why coaches and trainers watch their computers is that many athletes wear technologically advanced uniforms that ₂₀ monitor their activities. Perhaps some of the most well-known advances are computer chips that are placed inside shoes or affixed to them or the bibs that athletes wear. These chips relay messages to a geo-positioning system and tell the officials of an event at what time each runner has crossed each stage of a race. ₂₅ With this technology, coaches know where a runner is along a

particular course, or whether a runner has stopped running for any reason.

Many athletes now have special lightweight shirts that not only
30 absorb sweat and moisture from their bodies but also monitor
their heart rate and respiration. Additionally, the athlete's posture
can be determined by the shirt. Traditional sports socks help
absorb perspiration and cushion the feet. However, new high-
tech socks can monitor the speed and weight distribution of an
35 athlete. Also, these socks can detect how many steps the athlete
or wearer has taken, acting very much like a pedometer.

(39) These advances in sports technology are only just beginning.
However, it is evident that this kind of sportswear is making
certain kinds of monitoring and certain analytical devices
40 unnecessary. Athletes and their coaches will benefit from such
sportswear. So the next time you see an athlete donning a bright,
colorful uniform, remember that although fashion designers might
have designed the way it looks, scientists and engineers have
designed the way it functions in the hope that each athlete may
45 be able to perform at his or her top level.

(441 words)

1 次の(1)から(5)に続くフレーズとして最も適切なものを下の①から⑤より選びなさい。なお、①から⑤は1回しか使えません。

_____ (1) Athletes spend

_____ (2) Coaches and trainers would

_____ (3) Traditional sports socks help

_____ (4) It is evident that

_____ (5) These chips relay messages

① absorb perspiration and cushion the feet.

② the sportswear is a kind of monitoring system.

③ countless hours training.

④ to a geo-positioning system.

⑤ monitor athletes by visual observation.

2 次の(1)から(5)の英文がそれぞれ正しい意味を表すように、和文を参考にして( )に入れる最も適切な語句を下の①から⑩より選びなさい。なお、①から⑩は1回しか使えません。

_____ (1) きつい練習とトレーニングはどの運動選手にとっても必要不可欠です。

Hard work and training are ( ) for every athlete.

_____ (2) 運動選手の姿勢さえもシャツによって決められます。

The athlete's ( ) can be determined by the shirt.

_____ (3) 運動選手も彼らのコーチもこのようなスポーツウェアから恩恵を受けています。

Athletes and their coaches will ( ) from such sportswear.

_____ (4) 皆さんは運動選手が明るい色のカラフルなユニフォームを着用しているのを見ることでしょう。

You can see an athlete ( ) a bright, colorful uniform.

_____ (5) 技術者は、どの運動選手も自分の力を出し切ることができるかもしれないと願って、設計しているのです。

Engineers have designed the way it functions in the ( ) that each athlete may be able to perform at his or her top level.

| ① critical | ② crucial | ③ post | ④ posture | ⑤ benefit |
| ⑥ business | ⑦ putting | ⑧ wishing | ⑨ hope | ⑩ donning |

3 本文の内容について下記の設問に日本語で答えなさい。

(1) 運動選手をサポートする専門家たちにはどのような人たちがいますか。

_____

(2) コーチやトレーナーが運動選手の調子を観察する方法はどのように変化してきていますか。

昔 _____

今 _____

(3) 運動選手の靴に埋め込まれたチップはどのような働きをしますか、二つあげなさい。

① _____

② _____

(3) 運動選手の着ている最新のシャツや靴下にはどのような機能が備わっていますか、それぞれまとめなさい。

shirts _____

_____

socks _____

_____

Discussion, Paragraph Writing, Presentation

Questions for Discussion

1. What is your favorite sport to watch? Why? What is your favorite sport to play? Why?
2. Do you like individual sports, like tennis or badminton, or team sports, like soccer or baseball?
3. What ways can these sports clothes be used for sick people at home or in hospitals?
4. Besides making clothing using state-of-the-art technology, what other ways is technology used in sports training and sporting events?
5. Who is your favorite Japanese athlete? Why?

Pair Practice

A
1. I spent countless hours studying for my entrance examination.
3. We bought lightweight jackets that really keep us warm in the winter.
5. My grandfather wore a heart monitor that collected data each day from his heart.
7. Chips in shoes can send signals to a GPS to show where a runner is in a race.

B
2. Our club has financial sponsors to help us buy telescopes for our observation of the stars.
4. My new high-tech watch monitors my heart beat and rate of breathing when I work out.
6. Our rugby team hired two coaches from New Zealand to help the members train for the tournament.
8. These new shirts change colors if a patient gets a fever, and that helps the nurses monitor them.

Presentation Skills

Give a 1-minute presentation about your favorite sport or athlete.

3-D Printers / History of Printers

3Dプリンタ　プリンタの歴史

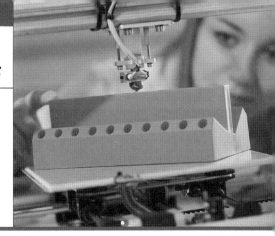

到達目標
□ 英英辞典を参照することができる。
□ プリンタの歴史について説明できる。

事前学習　次の単語を予習して授業を受けましょう。

A　次の(1)から(10)の単語の訳として最も適切な日本語をそれぞれ①から③より、選びなさい。

____ (1) matter [① 物質 ② 原料 ③ 事件]
____ (2) describe [① 記述する ② 賛成する ③ 印刷する]
____ (3) reverse [① 反対する ② 変える ③ 裏返しにする]
____ (4) character [① 文字 ② 文学 ③ 成果]
____ (5) bake [① 焼く ② 固める ③ 溶かす]
____ (6) clay [① レンガ ② 泥 ③ 粘土]
____ (7) improve [① 改良する ② 加熱する ③ 燃やす]
____ (8) process [① 現象 ② 加工する ③ 導体]
____ (9) durable [① 柔軟性のある ② 耐性のある ③ 曲げやすい]
____ (10) revolve [① 回転する ② 再生する ③ 持ち運ぶ]

B　次の(1)から(10)の日本語の意味にあう最も適切な英語を①から③より選びなさい。

____ (1) 鉄 [① steel ② iron ③ alloy]
____ (2) 起源とする [① originate ② origin ③ original]
____ (3) 進化する [① evolve ② evoke ③ evaporate]
____ (4) 似ている [① smile ② similar ③ unlike]
____ (5) 足す [① add ② put ③ foot]
____ (6) 引く [① submit ② subtract ③ subscribe]
____ (7) 積み上げる [① decide ② deposit ③ decrease]
____ (8) 糊、接着剤 [① glue ② bind ③ fond]
____ (9) 規準、標準 [① stand ② standard ③ complete]
____ (10) 回路 [① circle ② circuit ③ cycle]

(42) "Printed material or matter." This is a term that has been used for many years to describe books, newspapers, comic books, works of visual art such as photographs, or perhaps even sheet music. Printed matter was and is produced by printers. It is said that the first printers originated in China. Chinese characters were reversed and hand-carved into wood, and that wood was then used to print written material. Later, the Chinese created moveable type printers with characters or individual letters made from baked clay and then placed into an iron frame for printing. These character blocks could be used many times.

Over the years, the movable type printer with clay blocks was improved, and the wood was processed to make it more durable. Additionally, a revolving table was used to help increase the efficiency and speed of the printing process. Over the years, printing presses and printers have continued to develop and evolve. Ink-jet and laser printers are now commonly found in almost any office, and the technology continues to improve as speed, clarity and high definition printing have become standards all printers must meet.

(43) The evolution of the printing press and printers has become the subject of study for many mechanical engineers. One mechanical engineer, Professor Ely Sachs, was fascinated with integrated circuits, casting molds and inkjet printing heads back in the 1980s. Professor Sachs was initially working on a process to produce integrated circuits made by a planar process where patterns of material are added or subtracted from the initial layer

of silicon used for the circuit. This process gave him the idea
that similar techniques could be used to print other things. Sachs
came up with the concept of "Binder jetting", where layers of
30 metal are deposited and then held together with a binding agent
or type of glue to print a complete part. Professor Sachs studied
both laser printers and ink-jet printers and realized that, although
laser printers were quite fast and efficient, the heat from the
lasers could cause damage to the images being printed. For that
35 reason, he focused his studies on the ink-jet printing head.

44 Professor Sachs is one of many that have had a role in the
evolution of printers used to reproduce the printed word into
printers which produce many different things. Prosthetic arms
and legs for children, car parts, and even houses are all now
40 things that are being printed by 3-D printers. With all these
developments and with all the products being made by 3-D
printers, it may be time for the definition of "printed material
or matter" also to evolve to keep up with the advancement in
printing seen in the past 40 years.

(448 words)

Notes
l. 6   reversed and hand-carved   反転されて手で彫られた
l. 25   planar process   平面プロセス

Exercises

1 次の(1)から(5)までの各英語の説明に相当する最も適切な語を下の①から⑩より選びなさい。なお、①から⑩は1回しか使えません。

_____ (1) skillfully made by hand, not by machine

_____ (2) a chemical substance that exists as a solid or as a powder and is used to make glass, bricks, and parts for computers

_____ (3) a hollow container that you pour a liquid or soft substance into, so that when it becomes solid, it takes the shape of the container

_____ (4) the quality of doing something well and effectively, without wasting time, money, or energy

_____ (5) an artificial leg, tooth, or other part of the body which takes the place of a missing part

① silicon	② rubber	③ clay	④ mold	⑤ cast
⑥ prosthesis	⑦ efficiency	⑧ affect	⑨ hand-carved	⑩ bind

2 次の各和文の意味を表すように、①から⑦を並べかえて最も適切な英文を作りなさい。

(1) 最初のプリンタは中国で発明されたと言われています。
It [① that ② the ③ printer ④ was ⑤ said ⑥ first ⑦ is] invented in China.

(2) 今では、プリンタはどこの家庭でも見られます。
Now [① printers ② found ③ almost any ④ in ⑤ are commonly ⑥ home].

(3) ある教授は集積回路に夢中でした。
One [① with ② was ③ the ④ circuits ⑤ integrated ⑥ fascinated ⑦ professor].

(4) 彼は新しいプリンターの概念を思いつきました。

He [① with ② new ③ of ④ the ⑤ came ⑥ concept ⑦ up] the printer.

(5) 彼はプリンターの開発と発展において重要な役割を果たしました。

He [① an ② in ③ role ④ played ⑤ important ⑥ the evolution and development ⑦ has] of the printer.

3 次の(1)から(5)までの英文で本文の内容に合致しているものには ① (= true)を、異なっているものは ② (= false)を書きなさい。

_____ (1) Printed matter does not include photographs and visual arts.

_____ (2) The first printers originated in China were used in many countries.

_____ (3) The round table enabled people to develop the new type of mobile printer.

_____ (4) One professor invented a 3-D printer which produces many different things such as car parts or houses.

_____ (5) 3-D printers are not developed from the laser printers.

4 次の問いに英語で答えなさい。

(1) What is printed matter?

It is _____.

(2) Who is Professor Sachs?

He is _____.

Discussion, Paragraph Writing, Presentation

Questions for discussion:

1. Can you name three ways that 3-D printers are changing the field of commerce? Medicine? Architecture?
2. Do you think that individuals should be able to buy and use 3-D printers in their homes and places of work?
3. Do you like to read manga as printed matter or in electronic form? Why?
4. Professor Sachs improved an "old" way of printing to make 3-D printing. Can you think of something "old" in your daily life that could be improved into something "new" and better?

Pair Dictation Practice

A 1. My parents still like to read the newspaper as printed matter, but I like to read it on my tablet.
3. The factory has one of the highest efficiency rates in the country.
5. Gasoline powered engines have evolved into electrical or hybrid engines.

B 2. Printing presses used just a few years ago were very big and noisy.
4. My father just bought a large high definition television so my family can watch movies together.
6. The runner, who won the race, has a brand new prothesis made by a 3-D printer.

Presentation Skills:

Give a 60 second presentation to your group and explain how something you use in your everyday life works. For example, how does a mechanical pencil work? How does a stapler work? How does a hair dryer work?

Drones

ドローン

到達目標

☐ パラグラフごとに内容を確認しながら読むことが
できる。

☐ ドローンの歴史、用途について説明できる。

事前学習 次の単語を予習して授業を受けましょう。

A 次の(1)から(10)の単語の訳として最も適切な日本語をそれぞれ①から③より、選びなさい。

____ (1) captain 　　　　[① 統率する 　② 連れていく 　③ 帽子をかぶる]

____ (2) operate 　　　　[① 操作する 　② 支える 　③ 扱う]

____ (3) maneuver 　　　[① 手で作る 　② 介護する 　③ 操縦する]

____ (4) generate 　　　 [① 使う 　② 発電する 　③ 成り立つ]

____ (5) amaze 　　　　 [① 悩ます 　② 溶かす 　③ 驚かす]

____ (6) foresee 　　　　[① 予測する 　② 成功する 　③ 固める]

____ (7) license 　　　　[① 免許証 　② 出陣 　③ 壊す]

____ (8) deliver 　　　　 [① 工夫する 　② 分割する 　③ 配送する]

____ (9) combat 　　　　[① 戦う 　② 想像する 　③ 飛ぶ]

____ (10) inspect 　　　 [① 予告する 　② 検査する 　③ 運ぶ]

B 次の(1)から(10)の日本語の訳として最も適切な英語をそれぞれ①から③より、選びなさい。

____ (1) 漏れ 　　　[① leak 　② pipe 　③ purpose]

____ (2) 緊急 　　　[① essential 　② emission 　③ emergency]

____ (3) 軍事上の 　[① military 　② mechanical 　③ electrical]

____ (4) 証明する 　[① prove 　② pride 　③ proof]

____ (5) 発明 　　　[① invite 　② invention 　③ improve]

____ (6) 適切な 　　[① suitable 　② radioactive 　③ smooth]

____ (7) 増加する 　[① decrease 　② create 　③ increase]

____ (8) 輸送する 　[① transport 　② translate 　③ transmit]

____ (9) 貨物 　　　[① vehicle 　② cargo 　③ train]

____ (10) 無人の 　　[① unmanned 　② remote 　③ aerial]

(47)   Many young people look forward to getting their driver's license. Some people even train to get a license to captain a boat or pilot an airplane. People who operate these machines must have special skills to maneuver these machines and must receive special training to keep our roadways, waterways, and airways safe and accident free. However, there may come a day when drivers, captains and pilots will be replaced by remote, computerized devices. Such devices are called "drones".   5

    The idea of a drone and how it could help society began with Nikola Tesla. Tesla, a mechanical and electrical engineer, is most often known for his research in electricity and mechanical currents. He had many creative and important ideas regarding how to generate and use electricity. In 1894, Tesla showed the world the capability of wireless communication through radio waves, while in 1898, in New York's Madison Square Gardens, he amazed his audience by moving a small boat through a pool of water using only a remote-controller and radio waves.   10   15

(48)   Tesla, many years ago, was able to foresee a world which would utilize remote control vehicles. Tesla wrote, "The invention which I have described will prove useful in many ways. Vessels or vehicles of any suitable kind may be used, as life, dispatch, or pilot boats or the like, or for carrying letters packages, provisions, instruments, objects...".   20

    Since Tesla's small boat experiment, governments have used drones, or remote-controlled unmanned vehicles, for military   25 purposes. However, since 2006 drones have been used for non-military purposes. In times of emergencies, governments have used drones to deliver supplies to remote areas. Firefighters have used drones to help combat wildfires. Some companies now

30　inspect pipelines for leaks using pictures taken by drones.

(49)　Recently, the use of drones has increased even more. Private citizens have been able to obtain licenses to operate drones. Professional and amateur photographers use drones to take aerial pictures and videos. Delivery companies are beginning to

35　use drones to deliver packages. Taxi companies are considering placing drone-type technology in small helicopter-type vehicles to transport passengers from one place to another. And shipping companies are now considering using unmanned ships to transport cargo across the oceans.

40　Over the years, many children worldwide have enjoyed playing with radio-transmitted, remote-controlled toys – cars, boats, and robots, to name just a few – based very much on the ideas that Tesla showed the world in 1898. Over the next few years, this technology will surely change our ideas of transportation as well

45　as how we deliver products safely and efficiently to people all over the world.

(448 words)

Notes

l. 10　Nikola Tesla (1856-1943)　セルビア人。エジソンと並ぶ発明家。

Exercises

1 次の(1)から(5)までの各英語の説明に相当する最も適切な語を下の①から⑩より選びなさい。なお、①から⑩は1回しか使えません。

____ (1) the natural ability, skill, or power that makes a machine, person, or organization able to do something, especially something difficult

____ (2) a ship or large boat

____ (3) when you provide something that someone needs now or in the future

____ (4) to send someone or something somewhere for a particular purpose

____ (5) to get something that you want, especially through your own effort

① alloy	② vessel	③ provision	④ obtain	⑤ before
⑥ firefighter	⑦ delivery	⑧ utilize	⑨ capability	⑩ dispatch

2 次の各和文の意味を表すように、①から⑦を並べかえて最も適切な英文を作りなさい。

(1) 多くの若者が運転免許を取得するのを楽しみにしています。
Many [① people ② look ③ getting ④ their ⑤ to ⑥ forward ⑦ young] driver's license.

(2) 彼はリモートコントロールで動く車が利用できる世界を予見できていました。
He was [① able ② utilize ③ foresee ④ a world ⑤ which ⑥ would ⑦ to] remote control vehicles.

(3) 私が述べてきたこの発明は多くの点で有用であることを証明するでしょう。
The [① I have ② invention ③ will ④ described ⑤ useful ⑥ prove ⑦ which] in many ways.

(4) 配送会社は、小包を配送するためにドローンを使い始めています。

Delivery [① to ② are ③ use ④ to deliver ⑤ beginning ⑥ drones
⑦ companies] packages.

_____

(5) このテクノロジーは輸送に対する考え方を変化させるでしょう。

This [① change ② ideas ③ will ④ of ⑤ our ⑥ transportation
⑦ technology].

_____

3 次の(1)から(5)までの英文で本文の内容に合致しているものには ① (= true)を、
異なっているものは ②(= false)を書きなさい。

____ (1) We must have a special license to operate drones.

____ (2) Firefighters have used drones to help deliver packages.

____ (3) Nikola Tesla invented drones.

____ (4) Drones are a kind of remote and computerized device.

____ (5) In the future, drone-type technology is expected to transport
passengers.

4 次の問いに英語で答えなさい。

(1) According to the passage, how do photographers use drones?

They use drones to _____.

(2) Who was Nikola Tesla?

He was _____.

Discussion, Paragraph Writing, Presentation

Questions for Discussion

1. Do you think drones will replace delivery services?
2. Do you think drone ships will be safe on the ocean?
3. Do you have a drone? If so, is it easy to operate? What does it do?
4. Have you been to an event where drone photography was used?
5. Should everyone (anyone) be allowed to own a drone?

Pair Dictation

50 **A** 1. My grandfather worked at a small factory as a mechanical engineer.
   3. The electrical wattage in Europe is different than here in Japan.
   5. Many car companies are now developing inexpensive electric cars.
   7. The book I ordered was delivered by a small drone sent out by the delivery man.

51 **B** 2. I used to play with a remote-controlled airplane every day in the park.
   4. My aunt works in Kyushu as an electrical engineer.
   6. We put a smartphone in a drone and took pictures with it at our graduation.
   8. I saw a small helicopter taxi flying across the sky in Dubai.

Presentation Skills

Give a 1-minute presentation about your favorite toy in elementary school. What could it do? Can you still buy it now?

Problems with Plastics

プラスチックにかかわる問題

到達目標
□ 修飾関係に気をつけて読むことができる。
□ プラスチックにかかわる環境問題などについて説明
　できる。

事前学習　次の単語を予習して授業を受けましょう。

A　次の(1)から(10)の単語の訳として最も適切な日本語をそれぞれ①から③より、選びなさい。

_____ (1) drown 　　　　　[① 描く 　　② おぼれる 　③ 引きだす 　　]
_____ (2) pliable 　　　　　[① 固い 　　② しなやかな 　③ もろい 　　　]
_____ (3) definition 　　　[① 定義 　　② 決定的な 　③ 操作 　　　　]
_____ (4) chain 　　　　　[① 接着剤 　② 連鎖 　　③ 合金 　　　　　]
_____ (5) molecule 　　　[① 原子 　　② 分子 　　③ 原子核 　　　]
_____ (6) flexible 　　　　[① 柔軟な 　② 余裕のある 　③ 時間に正確な]
_____ (7) synthetic 　　　[① 自然な 　② 人口の 　③ 人造の 　　　]
_____ (8) ivory 　　　　　[① 象牙 　　② 粘土 　　③ 灰色 　　　　]
_____ (9) tusk 　　　　　[① きば 　　② えら 　　③ とげ 　　　　]
_____ (10) substance 　　[① 代替物 　② 物質 　③ 気体 　　　　]

B　次の(1)から(10)の日本語の訳として最も適切な英語をそれぞれ①から③より、選びなさい。

_____ (1) 頼る 　　　　　[① rely 　　② recycle 　③ remind 　　　　]
_____ (2) 信頼性 　　　　[① relieve 　② reliance 　③ reinforcement]
_____ (3) 解決 　　　　　[① solve 　② solution 　③ solvent 　　　]
_____ (4) 減らす 　　　　[① reduce 　② increase 　③ decline 　　　]
_____ (5) 分解する 　　　[① compose 　② decompose 　③ consist 　　]
_____ (6) 持続可能な 　　[① suitable 　② sustainable 　③ subtle 　　]
_____ (7) 汚染 　　　　　[① polite 　② polymer 　③ pollution 　　]
_____ (8) 燃料 　　　　　[① fuel 　　② fury 　　③ future 　　　　]
_____ (9) 説明する 　　　[① expose 　② exist 　③ explain 　　　]
_____ (10) 石油 　　　　　[① liquid 　② solid 　③ petroleum 　　　]

(52)   Plastics. We are drowning in a sea of plastic. Too many things are made of plastic or are put in plastic packaging. They are everywhere you look, and unfortunately they will be around for a very long time.

What is exactly plastic? At first, the word plastic meant   5
something that was pliable and easily shaped. Over the past 150 years, this definition has changed to include a group of materials called polymers. Polymer means "many parts" and polymers are made up of long chains of molecules. Polymers can be either natural or synthetic (man-made). The man-made polymers have   10
longer chains of molecules than the natural ones, and this is what makes them strong, lightweight and flexible.

(53)   In 1869, John Wesley Hyatt invented the first synthetic polymer. At that time, a company had said it would pay anyone who could create a material to take the place of ivory. Ivory   15
was used to make billiard balls, and since the game of billiards was very popular at that time, many elephants were being killed for their tusks. Mr. Hyatt treated a natural cellulose which came from cotton fiber with camphor. Through this experiment, Hyatt discovered a kind of plastic that could be molded into different   20
shapes. This new substance was very similar to tortoiseshell, horns, and ivory. Research continued, and about 40 years later, a totally man-made synthetic polymer was developed.

Since that time, we have been relying on man-made polymers for so many of our needs. Unfortunately, this reliance has come   25 with a cost. Synthetic polymers were made to help take a stress off of the environment, but as we have been using them for nearly everything, they are now destroying our environment.

(54) Scientists and engineers are now looking beyond synthetic
30 polymers and are exploring natural solutions to create new polymers. Some are looking at crops and plants for answers. If plants can be used, then the plastic / polymer industry can become more sustainable. Since plants are easily broken down in the environment, biodegradable bioplastics could help reduce the
35 environmental pollution created by plastics. Plants, not petroleum, can be used to make plastics - plastics which decompose easily after use. Other scientists are also researching ways to convert used plastics into fuel or energy sources for the future.

Over the past century and a half, our lives have become much
40 richer because of the role plastics and polymers have played. However, it is now time for us to examine our world and find new ways to make it a better, safer, and healthier place using the plastics and polymers of the future and not those of the past.

(438 words)

<u>Notes</u>

l. 8 polymer ポリマー
l. 18 cellulose セルロース
l. 19 camphor ショウノウ

Exercises

1 次の(1)から(5)までの各英語の説明に相当する最も適切な語を下の①から⑩より選びなさい。なお、①から⑩は1回しか使えません。

_____ (1) a solid substance such as wood, plastic, or metal

_____ (2) the smallest unit into which any substance can be divided without losing its own chemical nature

_____ (3) the people and things that are around you in your life

_____ (4) produced by combining different artificial substances

_____ (5) to change something into a different form

① molecule	② consider	③ building	④ synthetic	⑤ convert
⑥ environment	⑦ polymer	⑧ natural	⑨ atom	⑩ material

2 次の各和文の意味を表すように、①から⑦を並べかえて最も適切な英文を作りなさい。

(1) プラスチックの語は何か曲げやすいもの、容易に整形しやすいものを意味していました。
The word [① plastic ② that ③ meant ④ was ⑤ pliable ⑥ and ⑦ something] easily shaped.

(2) ポリマーは分子の長い鎖で作られています。
[① made ② long ③ of ④ Polymers ⑤ are ⑥ up ⑦ chains] of molecules.

(3) この新しい物質は。亀の甲羅によく似ていました。
This [① similar ② substance ③ very ④ was ⑤ to ⑥ new ⑦ tortoiseshell].

(4) 科学者たちはプラスチックを燃料に変える方法を研究し続けています。
Scientists [① researching ② convert ③ to ④ into ⑤ are ⑥ plastic ⑦ ways] fuel.

(5) 今や私たちが自分たちの世界を検証するときなのです。

It [① for ② is ③ us ④ examine ⑤ to ⑥ now time ⑦ our] world.

3

次の(1)から(5)までの英文で本文の内容に合致しているものには ① (= true) を、異なっているものは ② （= false）を書きなさい。

_____ (1) Plastic is made up of long chains of molecules.

_____ (2) We must not use plastic because of the environmental problems.

_____ (3) In the near future, problems with plastics will be solved by scientists' efforts.

_____ (4) Bioplastics can be broken down easily, and they will help reduce the environmental pollution.

_____ (5) It is not our responsibility that we use plastic too much.

4

次の問いに英語で答えなさい。

(1) According to the passage, why do plastics cause environmental problems?

Plastics are _____ .

(2) What was invented by John Wesley Hyatt?

_____ was invented.

Discussion, Paragraph Writing, Presentation

Questions for Discussion

1. What can we do to reduce plastic use in this school?   Rank the things we can do from EASY to DIFFICULT.
2. Plastic straws are being replaced with metal or paper straws. What about plastic bottles? How can we replace them?
3. Should there be a plastic tax placed on drinks and items placed in plastic?
4. What can be used instead of plastic to package food items or electronic goods?

Pair Dictation

A   1. The car's body is made from a pliable and lightweight material.
   3. Students walk around the neighborhood every day and pick up plastic trash.
   5. We are studying natural polymers in our biology class next semester.
   7. Many countries still rely heavily on fossil fuels to generate electricity.

B   2. Some scientists and medical doctors are exploring natural solutions once again to cure cancer.
   4. This new shopping bag is made of a new bioplastic so it is biodegradable.
   6. This designer only uses natural fibers and materials for his clothes.
   8. Scientists are looking at sustainable ways to solve the problems with plastics.

Summary Writing:

What are the key words in this article.   (Who? What? When? Why?) Use the key words to write a 30 to 50 word summary of this passage.

Usable Water for the World

この世界で使える水

到達目標

☐ パラグラフごとに内容のつながりを意識して読む
ことができる。

☐ 資源としての水について説明できる。

事前学習　次の単語を予習して授業を受けましょう。

| **A** | 次の(1)から(10)の単語の訳として最も適切な日本語をそれぞれ①から③より、選びなさい。 |

____ (1) abundance 　[① 劣化 　② 豊富 　③ 過剰 　]
____ (2) task 　[① 対策 　② 課題 　③ 荷物 　]
____ (3) usable 　[① 使える 　② 無用な 　③ 不可能な 　]
____ (4) reverse 　[① 正の 　② 逆の 　③ 中間の 　]
____ (5) impurity 　[① 純正 　② 発酵 　③ 不純物 　]
____ (6) shortage 　[① 余剰 　② 短絡 　③ 不足 　]
____ (7) pollutant 　[① 汚染物質 　② 清掃人 　③ 溶剤 　]
____ (8) remove 　[① 動かす 　② 取り除く 　③ 揺らす 　]
____ (9) irrigation 　[① イライラ 　② 水を引くこと 　③ 干ばつ 　]
____ (10) commercial 　[① 商業上の 　② 奉仕上の 　③ 選択上の 　]

| **B** | 次の(1)から(10)の日本語の意味にあう最も適切な英語を①から③より選びなさい。 |

____ (1) 蒸留 　[① distillation 　② desalination 　③ difference]
____ (2) 蒸気 　[① air 　② vapor 　③ boil]
____ (3) 液体 　[① gas 　② solid 　③ liquid]
____ (4) 効果的な 　[① efficient 　② effect 　③ effort]
____ (5) 適度の 　[① most 　② modest 　③ movement]
____ (6) 保守 　[① maintenance 　② economy 　③ machine]
____ (7) 据え付ける 　[① include 　② install 　③ increase]
____ (8) 手に入る 　[① reasonable 　② active 　③ available]
____ (9) 最近では 　[① nearly 　② later 　③ currently]
____ (10) おそらく 　[① possibly 　② possible 　③ impossible]

57   There is an abundance of water in the world, but one of the biggest tasks facing engineers today is how to make that water usable. Only 4% of the world's water is fresh and potable; the rest is salt water from the ocean. Unfortunately, salt water cannot be used for drinking, cleaning or even irrigation and   5 farming.

Scientists and engineers are helping people use more and more of the ocean's water. For example, many countries are already using desalinization plants to make salty water usable. Desalination is the process where salt is taken from seawater.   10 One of the ways this is done is by reverse osmosis. A membrane is used to separate the salt from the water. Unfortunately, a lot of energy is needed to complete this process. Also, desalination plants are very expensive to build, and so this process is not practical for the people who might need it the most.   15

58   Currently, engineers are exploring new processes. One consists of a filtering method using nano-osmosis. This process uses extremely small tubes of carbon called nanotubes. The size of these tubes is on the scale of nanometers, and they are excellent filters. When water is forced through these nanotubes, salt and   20 impurities are filtered out. These carbon nanotubes could help to solve the problem of water shortage in some areas.

Although desalination may help provide fresh drinking water for some people, it may still not be enough to solve the entire problem. Engineers and scientists are also looking at ways to   25 clean waste from water so that it can be recycled and reused. If impurities and pollutants can be removed from water, then that water could be used for irrigation and commercial uses.

59   Another method for providing clean water is water distillation.
30 When water is distilled, it is boiled to the point of becoming a vapor. The impurities in that water will remain behind so that when the vaporized water becomes liquid again, it is clean and usable. Small, efficient and economical distillation machines are being considered. Such distillation machines could possibly
35 provide water for a modest neighborhood at little cost.

Another engineering issue is the maintenance of water systems already in place. Many urban areas have very old or aging water systems. Aging pipes need to be replaced, and more efficient water systems need to be installed so that clean, fresh water will
40 always be available.

Clean, usable water is essential for all human beings. Scientists and engineers are currently working to solve the world's water problems, but until those problems are resolved, we can all help each other by conserving the water we use, one drop at a time.

(441 words)

Notes

l. 11   reverse osmosis   逆浸透圧法
l. 11   membrane   薄膜
l. 13   desalination   淡水化

1 次の(1)から(5)までの各英語の説明に相当する最も適切な語を下の①から⑩より選びなさい。なお、①から⑩は1回しか使えません。

____ (1) to make a liquid such as water or alcohol more pure by heating it so that it becomes a gas and then letting it cool.

____ (2) to discuss or think about something carefully

____ (3) to protect something and prevent it from changing or being damaged

____ (4) unwanted materials or substances that are left after you have used something

____ (5) a factory or building where an industrial process happens

① explore	② distill	③ boil	④ remain	⑤ resolve
⑥ conserve	⑦ drop	⑧ waste	⑨ filter	⑩ plant

2 次の各和文の意味を表すように、①から⑦を並べかえて最も適切な英文を作りなさい。

(1) 塩水は飲むためには用いることはできません。
[① water ② be ③ for ④ cannot ⑤ drinking ⑥ used ⑦ Salt].

(2) 飲用水を供給するためのもうひとつの方法は、水の蒸留です。
Another [① providing ② water ③ for ④ is ⑤ water distillation ⑥ clean ⑦ method].

(3) このプロセスは、ナノチューブと呼ばれる炭素の小さな管を使います。
This [① process ② small ③ tubes ④ carbon ⑤ of ⑥ uses ⑦ called] nanotubes.

(4) 多くの都市部ではとても年を経た水道システムを抱えています。

Many [① have ② systems ③ areas ④ very ⑤ aging ⑥ water
⑦ urban].

(5) 私たちは、使う水を大切に使うことでお互いを助けることができるのです。

We [① can ② other ③ help ④ by ⑤ the ⑥ conserving ⑦ each]
water we use.

3 次の(1)から(5)までの英文で本文の内容に合致しているものには ① (= true) を、
異なっているものは ② (= false) を書きなさい。

____ (1) Clean water is not always necessary for human beings.

____ (2) We should explore the ways for water distillation.

____ (3) We cannot drink salt water, but it is useful for farming.

____ (4) By filtering made of nanotubes, it is possible to get clean water from
salt water.

____ (5) Nanotubes enable us to drink water from the sea.

4 次の問いに英語で答えなさい。

(1) According to the passage, how do you keep water usable?

Our methods are _____ .

(2) What is the process of desalination?

Desalination is the process where _____

Discussion, Paragraph Writing, Presentation

Questions for Discussion

1. How can you reduce your water usage?
2. How can your field of study help resolve water problems around the world?
3. Do you think that bottled water should be sold in Japan? Why or why not?
4. Have you ever visited a place or area that was experiencing a water shortage? What did the people do there to prevent water from being wasted?

Pair Dictation

60 **A** 1. Japan has an abundance of fresh clean water.
   3. A desalination plant was built in the port city.
   5. The design for the new stadium was too expensive to build.
   7. My grandmother always used distilled water for her steam iron.

61 **B** 2. My apartment is very small but very efficient.
   4. This small machine can take the impurities out of the water.
   6. The government replaced all the water and sewage pipes after the earthquake.
   8. Farmers need fresh clean water for their vegetable crops.

Writing Practice

Write a 20 to 30 word description of this photo. Share your description with your group.

Origami Engineering

折り紙と技術

到達目標

☐ トピックセンテンスと指示文、具体例を意識して
　読むことができる。

☐ 折り紙と技術の関係について説明できる。

事前学習　次の単語を予習して授業を受けましょう。

A　次の(1)から(10)の単語の訳として最も適切な日本語をそれぞれ①から③より、選びなさい。

____ (1) fold 　　　　　　[　① 抱える 　　② 保つ 　　　③ 折る 　　　　]

____ (2) recognize 　　　[　① 認識する 　② 覚える 　　③ 忘れる 　　　]

____ (3) crane 　　　　　[　① 首 　　　　② 鶴 　　　　③ 犯罪 　　　　]

____ (4) technique 　　　[　① 手段 　　　② 技術 　　　③ 判断 　　　　]

____ (5) utilize 　　　　[　① 利用する 　② 監督する 　③ 廃棄する 　　]

____ (6) mathematics 　　[　① 物理学 　　② 数学 　　　③ 外科 　　　　]

____ (7) stretch 　　　　[　① 伸ばす 　　② たたむ 　　③ 縮める 　　　]

____ (8) influence 　　　[　① 効果 　　　② 結果 　　　③ 影響 　　　　]

____ (9) assemble 　　　[　① 解体する 　② 組み立てる ③ 固める 　　　]

____ (10) insert 　　　　[　① 挿入する 　② 吐き出す 　③ 溶かす 　　　]

B　次の(1)から(10)の日本語の意味にあう最も適切な英語を①から③より選びなさい。

____ (1) 正方形 　　[　① rectangle 　② square 　　③ triangle 　　　]

____ (2) 指示 　　　[　① support 　　② direction 　③ instruction 　]

____ (3) 複雑な 　　[　① compare 　② composition ③ complex 　　　]

____ (4) 曲げる 　　[　① bend 　　　② fall 　　　③ hang 　　　　　]

____ (5) 望遠鏡 　　[　① microscope ② telescope 　③ scope 　　　　]

____ (6) 災害 　　　[　① disaster 　② decrease 　③ distinguish 　]

____ (7) 機能 　　　[　① function 　② found 　　　③ fundamental 　]

____ (8) 供給 　　　[　① demand 　② supply 　　③ availability 　]

____ (9) 動機づける [　① courage 　② expire 　　③ inspire 　　　　]

____ (10) 配送する 　[　① deliver 　　② receive 　　③ package 　　　]

(62) Fold your square paper diagonally in half. Unfold it and now fold it diagonally in half in the other direction. Open the paper and turn it over. Now fold it horizontally in half. Do you recognize these instructions? These are the first steps in folding a paper crane. Yes, origami! 5

Origami is the traditional Japanese art technique of folding paper into different forms such as animals or flowers. When children learn how to fold paper into various objects, they learn that a 2D object - a piece of paper - can, through a few folds, become a 3D object. This technique, now recognized as origami 10 engineering, is being taught in many engineering programs around the world.

(63) Origami engineering is a field that utilizes the ideas and techniques of origami with applications in many different areas. Children may consider origami as merely a way to spend time 15 on a rainy day, but actually there are some very complex mathematical ideas behind origami. Origami folding techniques can help engineers design structures and machines that bend, stretch and even curve. As a result, engineers can solve some difficult problems by using origami. 20

For example, origami folding techniques have been used to make solar arrays compact enough to be taken into space. Once in space, the solar arrays are unfolded so that they may be utilized on satellites. Similar techniques have likewise been used to send telescopes into space; once they arrive at their 25 destination or orbit, they unfold to become telescopes through which scientists on the ground can view the universe.

(64)　　Another area where the influence of origami can be seen is in the creation of transformer-like robots. Engineers have been
30　able to build robots from panels that can self-assemble and move about on their own. Such robots could be sent into space or into remote or disaster areas to perform various functions - for example, to help in search and rescue efforts or to deliver supplies to those in need.

35　　In the medical field, origami techniques are being used by cardiovascular surgeons. Physicians can now insert a small folded balloon through a very thin catheter and place that balloon into a patient's clogged artery. Once properly positioned, the balloon can be inflated to help open up the patient's blockage.

40　　Origami, the traditional art of folding and unfolding paper to create an object from a simple piece of paper will continue to inspire engineers as they design and produce objects which assist us in our daily lives, both here on Earth and in space.

(421 words)

Notes
l. 22　solar array　太陽電池
l. 36　cardiovascular surgeons　心臓血管手術
l. 36　physician　医者
l. 37　balloon　風船
l. 37　thin catheter　細いカテーテル
l. 38　clogged artery　詰まった動脈
l. 39　inflate　膨張させる
l. 39　blockage　血管に詰まっているもの

Exercises

1 次の(1)から(5)までの各英語の説明に相当する最も適切な語を下の①から⑩より選びなさい。なお、①から⑩は1回しか使えません。

____ (1) a machine that has been sent into space and goes around the earth, moon, etc, used for radio, television, and other electronic communication

____ (2) the curved path travelled by an object which is moving around another much larger object such as the earth, the Sun, etc

____ (3) to save someone or something from a situation of danger or harm

____ (4) to carefully put something in a particular place

____ (5) a straight line that joins two opposite corners of a flat shape, usually a square

① diagonal	② unfold	③ direction	④ application	⑤ satellite
⑥ array	⑦ remote	⑧ rescue	⑨ orbit	⑩ position

2 次の各和文の意味を表すように、①から⑦を並べかえて最も適切な英文を作りなさい。

(1) この技法は世界中の多くの工学教育のプログラムで教えられつつあります。
This [① is ② many ③ technique ④ taught ⑤ engineering ⑥ in ⑦ being] programs around the world.

(2) 子供たちはいろいろな形に紙を折る方法を学びます。
Children [① how ② paper ③ fold ④ to ⑤ into ⑥ learn ⑦ various] objects.

(3) 技術者たちは、折り紙を使って難しい問題を解決することができます。
Engineers [① difficult ② can ③ problems ④ using ⑤ solve ⑥ by ⑦ origami].

(4) 折り紙のたたむ技術は太陽電池を小さくするためにも使われてきました。

Origami [① been ② to ③ have ④ solar arrays ⑤ make ⑥ folding techniques ⑦ used] compact.

(5) 技術者たちは日常生活で私たちを支えてくれるものの設計と制作をしています。

Engineers [① which ② us ③ objects ④ our daily ⑤ in ⑥ design and produce ⑦ assist] lives.

---

3 次の問いに日本語で答えなさい。

(1) According to the passage, how do you fold a paper crane?

(2) How do engineers use origami techniques in the field of robot engineering?

---

4 次の問いに英語で答えなさい。

(1) According to the passage, what is origami?

Origami is _____ .

(2) What are the applications of origami techniques in designing structures and machines?

Origami techniques are used to _____

Discussion, Paragraph Writing, Presentation

Questions for Discussion

1. Origami is a traditional craft from Japan. Can you think of other traditional arts or crafts from Japan that can be used by engineers and scientists?
2. When did you learn how to do origami? Who taught you? What was the first thing you learned how to fold?
3. How do you think origami engineering can be used in the future? Explain.

Pair Dictation

65 **A** 1. Fold your paper in half. Now open it up and fold it again the other way.
3. The new telescope can be folded up to fit in a small space.
5. The Japanese satellite is used to take photos of the universe.
7. The research team is developing a robot to help search for people who get lost hiking in the jungle.

66 **B** 2. Origami is a traditional craft from Japan.
4. Researchers are working on new techniques to help doctors treat patients in remote areas.
6. This transformer toy folds up into a small boat.
8. The horizontal axis shows the number of cars sold.

Writing and Presentation

Write the instructions on how to make something using origami.
After you write these instructions, read them aloud to your classmates.
Have your classmates fold their paper according to your instructions.
Were they successful?

Global Engineering

グローバルエンジニア

到達目標

☐ 筆者の主張について論理構成を意識して読むことが
できる。

☐ グローバル化と技術者の関係について説明できる。

事前学習　次の単語を予習して授業を受けましょう。

A　次の(1)から(10)の単語の訳として最も適切な日本語をそれぞれ①から③より、選びなさい。

____ (1)　respect 　　　　[　① うらやむ　　② 従う　　　　③ 尊敬する　]

____ (2)　observe 　　　　[　① 認める　　　② 観察する　　③ 預ける　]

____ (3)　concept 　　　　[　① 概要　　　　② 概算　　　　③ 概念　]

____ (4)　confront 　　　　[　① 直面する　　② 考慮する　　③ 攻撃する　]

____ (5)　venture 　　　　[　① 試す　　　　② 指示する　　③ 許す　]

____ (6)　workforce 　　　[　① 作業所　　　② セミナー　　③ 労働力　]

____ (7)　specific 　　　　[　① 特別の　　　② 科学の　　　③ 種の　]

____ (8)　collaborate 　　[　① 作業する　　② 協働する　　③ 比較する　]

____ (9)　approve 　　　　[　① 是認する　　② 非難する　　③ 抑える　]

____ (10)　manufacture 　[　① 生産する　　② 工業化する　③ 破壊する　]

B　次の(1)から(10)の日本語の意味にあう最も適切な英語を①から③より選びなさい。

____ (1)　技能　　　　[　① skull　　② skill　　　③ sketch　]

____ (2)　能力　　　　[　① able　　② ability　　③ available　]

____ (3)　最終的には　[　① final　　② last　　　③ finally　]

____ (4)　発生する　　[　① happen　② explode　　③ explore　]

____ (5)　会社　　　　[　① country　② county　　③ company　]

____ (6)　ある種の　　[　① curtain　② certain　　③ kindness　]

____ (7)　共有する　　[　① shield　② settle　　③ share　]

____ (8)　特有の　　　[　① party　② superior　　③ particular　]

____ (9)　工場　　　　[　① industry　② experiment　③ factory　]

____ (10)　未来　　　　[　① function　② fact　　　③ future　]

(67)   "Global". "Globalism". "Globalization". These are all words you have seen or heard in textbooks, on television and on the Internet. What makes an engineer or scientist "global"? What skills do engineers need to work in today's global industry? Is it the ability to speak a foreign language? 5

   To become a global engineer, there are several things that engineering students should do. First, to work with engineers and people from other cultures, an engineer should first understand his or her own culture. When someone understands their own culture, they will be able to respect and learn from other 10 people and different cultures. Global engineers should also have experience in another country or culture. Going to a different country gives a person a chance to observe and experience many different things, ways of life, and ideas. Finally, a global engineer should have a good understanding of both the history 15 of our world as well as the concept of globalization. Global engineers recognize the ways we are all interconnected, and from this interconnectedness can come solutions to the problems confronting today's world.

(68)   As engineers venture into the global workforce, they are 20 realizing that there is a lot to be learned from engineers from other cultures and countries. Problems may be the same, but the way they look at those problems may be quite different and the way to solve the problems may also be quite different.

25   Global projects are happening more and more. The Boeing
     Dreamliner airplane is one such project. Boeing, located in the
     United States, decided to ask engineers and companies all around
     the world to help make the best airplane possible. Before the
     Dreamliner, Boeing asked companies to build a specific part in
30   a certain way. With the Dreamliner, Boeing engineers began to
     ask engineers around the world to collaborate with them. Boeing
     shared what it needed in a particular part, like a wing, a window
     or even chair. Then engineers in one area would begin designing
     the part, and after much discussion with other engineers at
35   Boeing and around the world, the final part would be approved.
     The manufacturing of the various parts of the plane, like the
     designing, would take place in many factories around the world.
     Once manufactured, the parts are sent to one factory and the
     Dreamliner is put together in a very short amount of time.

69   Global engineering collaboration has created one of the most
     environmentally friendly, economical, spacious and safe airplanes
     ever to be flown in the sky. It is a "dream come true" for global
     engineers, and an example of just how important global engineers
     working together will be for the future of our world.

                                                        (444 words)

Exercises

1 次の(1)から(5)までの各英語の説明に相当する最も適切な語を下の①から⑩より選びなさい。なお、①から⑩は1回しか使えません。

_____ (1) affecting or including the whole world

_____ (2) the large-scale production of goods or of substances such as coal and steel

_____ (3) to put or build something in a particular place

_____ (4) to make a drawing or plan of something that will be made or built

_____ (5) a carefully planned piece of work to get information about something, to build something, to improve something etc

① industry	② foreign	③ global	④ decide	⑤ project
⑥ locate	⑦ airplane	⑧ design	⑨ wing	⑩ interconnect

2 次の各和文の意味を表すように、①から⑦を並べかえて最も適切な英文を作りなさい。

(1) これらは全てインターネット上で見聞きした言葉です。
These [① seen ② all words ③ on ④ you ⑤ or heard ⑥ are ⑦ have] the Internet.

(2) 工学を学んでいる学生がすべきことがいくつかあります。
There [① that ② several ③ engineering students ④ do ⑤ should ⑥ are ⑦ things].

(3) 人々のあれらの問題に対する見方は全く異なっているかもしれない。
The [① be ② at ③ they ④ those problems ⑤ may ⑥ look ⑦ way] quite different.

(4) 私たちの会社は最高の製品を可能にするのを手伝っています。
Our [① help ② companies ③ make ④ products ⑤ possible ⑥ best ⑦ the].

(5) グローバルに活躍するエンジニアが一緒に働くことはどれだけ重要かという一つの例が未来のためになるでしょう。
An [① global engineers ② will be ③ working together ④ example of ⑤ how important ⑥ the future ⑦ for].

3 次の問いに日本語で答えなさい。

(1) According to the passage, what is important for globalization?

(2) What should you do to become a global engineer?

4 次の問いに英語で答えなさい。

(1) According to the passage, what should a global engineer have a good understanding of?

He or she should have a good understanding of _____.

(2) What is global engineering collaboration?

It is _____

Discussion, Paragraph Writing, Presentation

Questions for Discussion

1. What is the difference between "globalization" and "internationalization"?
2. What do you think is the most important trait needed to be a global engineer?
3. Can you name three products that are the result of global engineering?
4. What industry is very global now?
5. Should engineers learn more than one foreign language?
6. Should engineering students study abroad?

Pair Dictation

A 70
1. These engineers are collaborating with a team from Europe, so they work at strange hours.
3. I went out to dinner with friends from India and learned how to eat curry with my hand.
5. Next summer, I am going to go backpacking in South East Asia.

B 71
2. My seminar group will travel to Taiwan to collaborate with students at a national university there.
4. I am interested in how students learn math in India.
6. My dream is to work for a global company that develops train systems for places all over the world.

Paragraph writing

Write a short paragraph (50 to 70 words) about education for global engineers.

Presentation Skills

If you could go anywhere in the world, where would you go? Describe your dream trip and how it will help you in your future. (45 seconds to 1 minute)

４技能を伸ばす理工系学生のための基礎英語

| 検印
省略 | ©2020 年 1 月 31 日　第 1 版発行 |

編著者	奥　聡一郎
	Lisa Gayle Bond
発行者	原　雅久
発売所	株式会社 朝日出版社

101-0065　東京都千代田区西神田 3-3-5
電話（03）3239-0271
FAX（03）3239-0479
e-mail: text-e@asahipress.com
振替口座　00140-2-46008
組版・Office haru ／製版・錦明印刷

乱丁、落丁本はお取り替えいたします
ISBN 978-4-255-15653-8 C1082